Ethics in Business:

A Literature Review

by

Alan Lovell

Published by
The Institute of Chartered Accountants of Scotland
CA House, 21 Haymarket Yards, Edinburgh EH12 5BH

First Published 2005
The Institute of Chartered Accountants of Scotland

© 2005
ISBN 1 904574-16-5

Printed and bound in Great Britain
by T J International Ltd

CONTENTS

FOREWORD

In October 2004 the Research Committee of ICAS published *Taking Ethics to Heart*, an investigation into the ethical standing of accountants. It examined a number of remedies to ensure that appropriate mechanisms were in place to ensure 'good' decision making.

This literature review is the first in a series of three commissioned literature reviews associated with *Taking Ethics to Heart*. This review is published at a time when the ethical standing of accountants and corporations in the eyes of the general public continues to be an issue for the profession and the corporate world at large and when regulatory and professional bodies continue to seek solutions to these problems.

The literature review considers ethics in business from both an historical and contemporary perspective. The research considers the impact of globalisation and the respective responsibilities of corporations, consumers, communities and societies.

Part A of the literature review considers the historical development of ethics in business covering different geographical philosophical perspectives and identifies concepts central to an understanding of business in modern society. These central concepts are considered in turn and include the role of the market and the individual and the often conflicting interests and demands of business and the individual. These are considered in the light of changes in values and beliefs, including religion, over time.

Part B builds upon this analysis by considering contemporary issues in ethics in business. The report considers the concept and development of corporate social responsibility and the vested interests of stakeholders. The debate as to the extent corporations should be responsible for the non-economic impacts of their activity continues. The literature review then considers how this issue has been taken forward looking at the corporation as a citizen and the interplay between government and business. This reviews the power of multi-national corporations to influence social and political systems and the various codes of ethics that have been developed by corporations and other bodies.

The conclusions point to the need for business ethicists and business practitioners to begin debating the issues together. The issues to be debated include the interplay between possible changes by corporations to reflect more sustainable practices, the possible consequential need by consumers to accept higher prices and the role of governments to equalise prices using taxation and other policies.

The Research Committee of The Institute of Chartered Accountants of Scotland, through the auspices of the Scottish Chartered Accountants Trust for Education, has been happy to sponsor this project and is pleased that the literature review is becoming available at a time when the subject matter is so topical. The Committee recognises that the views expressed do not necessarily represent those of ICAS itself, but hopes that this project will contribute to the current debate on ethics in business.

David Spence
Convener
Research Committee
December 2005.

EXECUTIVE SUMMARY

Ethics in business has been an issue for as long as trade and commerce have taken place. The 'field' of business ethics is, however, of more recent vintage, possibly from around 1920 onwards (De George, 1987).

There is a clear relationship between 'ethics in business' and 'business ethics' for the latter is at one and the same time, commentator, critic, philosopher and prophet on the former. This literature review employs the phrase 'ethics in business' in its title, but draws upon various philosophical and empirical literature sources to identify and discuss key issues within the field.

Business ethics, is informed by rich and multiple sources including the literatures of philosophy (ethical, theological and legal), political economy, psychology, business and economics, and, importantly, day-to-day practice. The conjunction of philosophical arguments with everyday human practice, often within fraught and contradictory contexts, provides opportunities for new insights into the possibilities for moral agency at a variety of levels. Just as conceptions concerning the role and status of work have changed dramatically through time (as discussed below), so arguments relating to the 'virtuous life', bounded morality, the ethicality of competing economic and social systems, and the possibilities and desirability of universal (global) ethics add, at the very least, new contexts in which to debate classical ethical theories. At best, they might even influence the way particular classical theories are viewed. Business ethics embraces all of the theoretical perspectives mentioned above:

> while not being reducible to any of them … its object is the study of the morality and immorality as well as the possible justification of economic systems. (De George, 1987, p.204).

Part A of the literature review covers chapters one to five and these provide the background and context of the developing field of business ethics. The opening chapter considers how the literature base has grown and the different levels of analysis adopted by American, British and German writers, reflecting different philosophical perspectives. Chapters two, three and four focus upon different elements of the 'business ethics' debates. Initially the significance of 'the market' is the focus followed by the 'individual' and finally the role of 'values and virtues'. Chapter five concludes Part A, focusing upon the contribution of religious values and principles to business ethics debates.

Part B focuses upon contemporary business issues. Each of the chapters focuses upon different attempts and approaches to the ethical issues raised by contemporary businesses practices. Each chapter effectively deals with a different approach to trying to reduce, or at least, influence the power and practices of business corporations. Chapter six considers the concept of corporate social responsibility, whilst chapters seven and eight focus upon 'the stakeholder perspective' and 'the corporation as citizen' respectively. Chapter nine focuses upon government-business relationships, and the issues relating to globalisation are considered in this chapter, reflecting that the economic-social-political interplay is at its sharpest when globalisation issues are being considered. Chapter ten considers the attempts that have been made through corporate and intergovernmental organisations (IGO)-developed codes of ethics.

The penultimate and last substantive chapter considers a relatively new development in business ethics and the most robust attempt to-date, to develop an overarching and practical approach to understanding and developing coherent and inclusive business ethics policies and practices. This is known as Integrative Social Contract Theory. The final chapter provides a conclusion.

PART A

A CONSIDERATION OF THE HISTORICAL ROOTS OF ETHICS IN BUSINESS

CHAPTER ONE

HISTORICAL PERSPECTIVE

Introduction

De George (1987) began his analysis of the development of business ethics around 1920, but the mid-nineteenth century represents an important period of change as around this time the transition took place of the factory supplanting the home as the significant place of work (De George, 1987). With the attendant increase that this development afforded in terms of the control of labour, and with production able to be overseen in more obvious and detailed ways, issues of ethics and morality began to rear their heads in more significant and different ways (*eg* Braverman, 1974 and Keniston, 1986). In 1855 a significant development was enacted when the limited liability company was enshrined in statute in the UK, a development that was both a reaction to the financing problems of trade and industry and also to the formalisation of the dislocation of the owners of corporations from the day-to-day management of 'their' corporations.

It would be a misreading of history to suggest that the creation of limited liability status *caused* the dislocation between the owners and managers of corporations, because in the early to mid-nineteenth century many corporations were already of a size that required managers to be employed who were not members of the founding families or principal shareholders. This was despite the constraining effect of legislation that had been enacted as a response to earlier financial scandals[1]. The restrictive legislation of 'The Bubble Act' of 1719 was not repealed until 1825 and had acted as a brake upon organisational size and the capacity of companies to respond to developments in technology and trading opportunities.

In the early to mid-nineteenth century, controlling share ownerships (with unlimited liability) tended to be in the hands of individuals who would know the business tolerably well and who also had reasonably ready access to 'their' corporation (Aranya, 1984). However, Aranya (1984, pp.265/266)) observed that prior to 1844 "legislation generally protected the directors and managers at the expense of the shareholders". Lee (1984) and Edey (1984) also referred to the manipulation of company accounting information by managers at the expense of the owners' interests during the early nineteenth century, indicating that concerns over corporate governance have had a long history.

Another interesting development was that, as Chandler (1996) observed, that by 1900 it was becoming easier to rise to positions of economic influence through the newly centralised management structures of the large corporations than by owning one's own business. "This pattern was already clear in the railroads, the nation's first business bureaucracies" (Chandler, 1996, pp.66/67).

The concerns over corporate governance continued to rumble on, although De George (1987) argued that the development of business ethics as a field of enquiry did not effectively begin until around 1920. Different writers analyse the development of the field of business ethics in different ways. De George suggests that the field can be analysed, at least at the time he was writing, into five phases, whilst Epstein (1989) chooses a four-part categorisation. However, both writers commence their analysis at around the same time. In terms of De George's analysis the first period covers the years from around 1920 through to 1960. During this period the emphasis was primarily theological and religious (Carlen, 1981), with the social encyclicals of the Popes raising questions about just wages and the morality of capitalism. Influential amongst those contributing to the business ethics debates of the day were Messner (1952) and Niebuhr (1932), the latter being described by De George as, "the most important and influential of this period, [whose] critique of capitalism was trenchant and provocative" (De George, 1987).

Carey (1984) refers to the contribution of William Z Ripley, a Harvard professor, who, in the early 1920s wrote about the "docility of corporate shareholders permitting themselves to be honeyfuggled" and, in relation to the public utilities industries, of "the hoodwinking of the shareholders" (p.243). Of accountants Ripley observed, "accountants are enabled to play ball with figures to an astounding degree" (Carey, 1984). Thus, the concerns over corporate governance identified by Edey (1984) and Lee (1984), mentioned above, continued on through the latter part of the nineteenth century and into the early part of the twentieth century, culminating in Berle and Means (1932) seminal publication. In the preface, Berle and Means (1932) give credit to Ripley for his pioneering work on issues of corporate governance. Thus, in this opening period of business ethics, the concerns were centred around issues of corporate governance, but concerns about corporate power were also powerfully raised by Niebuhr (1932) and the exploitative and alienating tendencies of the capitalist system.

Environmental issues

The second of De George's periods of analysis, the 1960s, were seen as a distinct period as it represented the rise of public expressions of disquiet over social issues and, particularly, ecological and environmental issues. The business ethics publications of this period were described as 'reactive rather than systematic' (De George, 1987) as the focus tended to be upon specific cases, rather than attempting to consider what these specific examples might say of the broader systems' issues. Given that most of the literature at this time was by American writers, the focus upon individual cases supports Enderle's (1996) analysis that the primary focus of American writers has tended to be at the individual level.

Notwithstanding the 1960s being classified as a period of growing public articulateness about the social and ecological impacts of corporate activity, the cases that have become exemplars of the corporate impact on the environment did not come to the public's attention until post 1970 such as The Love Canal case (Mescon and Vozikis, 1984); The Reserve Mining Company; the depositing of taconite waste into Lake Superior (Matthews *et al.* 1985), and the Bhopal accident (Fisher and Lovell, 2003). More recently, the cases of Shell's operations in Nigeria (Newberry and Gladwin, 2002) and the Exxon Valdez disaster (Buchholz and Rosenthal, 1998), underscore that the environmental impact of business operations remains a consistent issue, particularly if senior business people hold the belief that the business sphere operates with different norms from the other spheres of human activity (Walzer, 1983). The following quote from Carr (1968) is well-documented, but is nonetheless worth repeating for it represents a perspective that some business people still formally articulate, whilst others appear to support in their actions, if not their words.

> *A good part of the time the businessman is trying to do to others as he hopes others will not do unto him … The game* [poker] *calls for distrust of the other fellow. It ignores the claim for friendship. Cunning, deception and concealment of one's strength and intentions, not kindness and open-heartedness, are vital in poker. And no-one should think any worse of the game of business because its standards of right and wrong differ from the prevailing traditions of morality in our society.* (Carr, 1968, pp.145-146).

The Carr perspective views any utterance by a business executive in support of corporate social responsibility as either a tactical ploy or an expression of naivety that will only lead to business failure. If businesses are to modify their actions with respect to environmental issues then the

Carr position is that it will only happen through compulsion, perhaps in the form of a tax that would be incorporated, in part or in whole, *via* increased prices. This is the approach argued by Ruff (1985) as being the only realistic hope of changing corporate behaviour with respect to social and environmental issues. Ruff's argument is not a clarion call for legislation that would impose or increase corporate taxes, but rather a claim that if left to business discretion, environmental protection would suffer as corporate and consumer behaviour was dictated by the price mechanism, and profit and growth motives.

This approach suits the preferences of market devotees because it leaves the market in its pre-eminent position as the determinant and manifestation of consumer behaviour, but it ignores the problems of information asymmetry between corporations and consumers and the ability of corporate power to affect political decision making such as influencing any proposed pollution taxes or restrictive legislation.

Two years after Carr's article, Milton Friedman (1970) published his seminal paper that remains to this day probably the most succinct defence of a 'free', capitalist-based market economy, drawing, in part, upon ethical reasoning to defend and justify his argument. Employing a different tack, Ackerman (1975) criticised pre-1971 writers for being devoid of sensitivity in understanding the difficulties of managing complex business organisations. Ackerman deflected criticism of corporate misbehaviour by arguing that examples of bad practice were very much the exception rather than the rule, and that even in the cases that had attracted criticism, more understanding needed to be displayed of the complexity of the decisions that executives had to take. Thus, the 1960s and the early 1970s were an important period of development in the business ethics debates, with the contributions beginning to reflect both criticisms and defences of corporate behaviour. Thirty years on from the publication of Friedman's 1970 paper, and in a rehearsal of Friedman's arguments, Wolf (2000) accused those (still) calling for greater corporate social responsibility as not only wishing to distort business activity, but also of confusing and misunderstanding the rationale of business. Wolf was dismissive of those demanding greater social responsibility from corporations with respect to vulnerable eco-systems and social systems. The role of well run companies was to make profits, Wolf argued, not save the planet.

Business ethics

The 1970s are marked out by De George as the third distinct phase in the development of 'business ethics' because it was during this period that contributions began to appear from philosophers and political economists on the subject of business ethics. For the first time the 'field' of business ethics emerged as a subject. The most notable contribution during this period was that of Rawls (1971, revised in 1999), whose arguments concerning the notions of justice were extremely influential. Contributions continued from writers approaching the subject from a business perspective, but now these contributions began to draw upon the work of Rawls and others, such as: Jones (1977); La Croix (1976) who employed Thomistic ethics to defend his arguments; Steiner (1975); and Steiner and Steiner (1977). By the close of the 1970s De George (1987) argued that business ethics existed even though there was little agreement as to precisely what it was.

The fourth of De George's periods was that from 1980 to 1985, during which time no new public issues arose, but the strength of the business ethics literature base increased significantly and in so doing began to shed its primarily academic location. Its possible contribution to business and social life was increasingly recognised and debates on business ethics moved into the world of practice.

The fifth and final phase of De George's analysis, post 1985, was represented by an agenda for action. Interestingly, De George (1987) observed that:

In the United States the easy work has already been done [on business ethics]. *The obvious problems have been raised and the obvious positions stated. Basic introductions have been written and anthologies assembled* (p.206).

His agenda identified seven areas upon which he felt that those concerned with business ethics should concentrate their efforts if business ethics was to move forward. The seven areas that De George identified can be grouped into two main concerns. The first was associated with academic programmes, both undergraduate and (the then developing area of) postgraduate education. De George's argument was that ethics in general, and business ethics in particular, could be taught, or that at least business education that possessed a strong ethical base could and would stimulate ethical awareness and sensitivity. The second major concern was the need for higher quality, more robust empirical research that encompassed more inter-disciplinary research, with a greater cooperation and involvement between academics and business practitioners. De George was keen to celebrate good practice and to study the conditions that allowed a discussion on ethical issues to flourish and for ethical practice to become the norm in business organisations.

As a guide to future researchers De George suggested a three-part classification to facilitate applied research: the micro or individual level of analysis, such as individual, personal dilemmas; the macro organisational level of analysis including price fixing, cartels, and pollution cases; and the systematic level, encompassing the connivance and duplicity of corporations, industries and governments to distort markets or act in ways that could not be seen as acting in the public interest, for example, the carving up of Indonesia following the fall of President Suharto, (Pilger, 2001). This three-part analysis was taken up by Enderle (1996), although Enderle changed the terminology slightly where the individual level was referred to as the micro, which was consistent with De George, but the organisational level of analysis was referred to as the meso level, and the systems level was referred to as the macro level. Notwithstanding these differences, the three-level categorisation is useful when considering the different emphases evident in the work of American, British and German writers on business ethics.

Contrasting perspectives on ethics and values

Business ethics in America, the UK and Germany, appear to have differing perspectives but it is not clear whether the differing levels of analysis reflected in the work of notable writers on business ethics in the three countries suggest any differences in ethics in business practice. Certainly, German corporate governance structures are distinct from those in American and British organisations, with two-tier boards, whilst the British and American preference is for unitary boards. However, the recommendations of the Higgs' Committee (2003) could be interpreted as a form of two-tier board approach by default[2], albeit with the two boards, in principle at least, having the interests of the shareholders as the primary/exclusive focus of their decision-making agendas.

Enderle (1996) and Hoffman (1998) argue that there is, on both sides of the Atlantic, a poor conceptualisation of business ethics. Multiple ideas abound, but there is no dominant theory or set of beliefs. As a kind of 'applied ethics', business ethics involves both empirical-analytical and normative-ethical dimensions.

Two dissimilarities stand out when contrasts are made between business ethics in America and in Continental Europe (Breidlid, *et al.* 1996; Hofstede, 1980; Rodgers, 1974; and Enderle, 1996). First, at the cognitive level, academics in Europe, particularly Germany and Scandinavia, are likely to weigh heavily the contributions that the social sciences can provide, but this emphasis is much less pronounced in the US. However, when the normative level is considered, Enderle

(1996) argues that North American academics draw upon a stronger acceptance of political and moral philosophy as a result of the work of people such as Rawls. This is a contestable assertion, given the long and notable history of German philosophers, such as Kant (Acton, 1970; Beck, 1965; Bowie, 1999); Leibnitz (Mates, 1983; Russell, 1900); Hegel (MacIntyre, 1972; Singer, 1983); Marx (McLellan, 1973; Singer, 1980); Engels (Tucker, 1978); Nietzsche (Nietzsche, 1973; Owen, 1995); and more recently Weber (1968); Husserl (1931, 1965); Heidegger (1959, 1978); and Habermas (1993), and the foundational or systems-level of analysis preferred by European writers on business ethics.

Enderle's (1996) second claim, that American academics are far more prepared to apply normative theories to real-world situations/ challenges and thus, "deal with normative issues in much more direct, open, and determined ways than do the 'reluctant' Europeans", is less contentious.

German academics are seen as mainly interested in foundational issues, such as conditions that might make possible notions of business ethics; the overall transformation of economic rationality; the synthesis of ethical and economic theories; the history of the relationship between ethics and economics; and the role of economic considerations in the foundation of ethics. These are less common areas of focus for American writers on business ethics, who tend to reflect the American belief in the superiority of market-based economics. The American perspective is seen as 'stronger' when normative, legal and ethical [philosophical] perspectives are considered where "a better balance and a complementary relationship between both seem to prevail in North America" (Enderle, 1996).

Enderle (1996), Mahoney (1990), and Marshall (1982), place the UK perspective on business ethics as much closer to the American position than that in Continental Europe, but with some notable differences on: matters of regulation; the status of the individual; and notions of freedom. An example of these differences in the level of

analysis is reflected in the work of Marshall (1982). He discussed
the debates in Germany, which, he argued, displayed a far more
reflective, historical perspective on economic developments than the
UK perspective. Marshall argued that in the early twentieth century
a central question in German academic and intellectual circles,
particularly the work of Weber (1968) was, 'What is it that is unique
about modern western capitalism?' In the UK, where the neo-classical
economic view was treated by many writers as a 'taken-for-granted'
assumption, there were few such questions. The German approach
posed further challenging questions, such as:

> ... *was economics to be an abstract, ahistorical discipline, based on a
> series of undemonstrated assumptions about economic phenomena and
> behaviour, notably that of the 'rational economic actor',* or [could it
> be] *an historical, concrete, empirical, and particular science, inductive
> and descriptive, rather than deductive and explanatory?* (Marshall,
> 1982, p.26).

Essentially Marshall was asking whether neo-classical economics,
founded on assumptions concerning 'rational economic man' could
ever become a 'realistic' and 'useful' discipline.

Weber came from the German 'Historical School' that saw
economic developments as critical elements, but set within historical
developments. Neo-classical economics, however, owed its existence
to deductive reasoning. The 'Historical School' stressed that, unlike
the subject matter of the natural sciences, society was in a continuous
process of evolution and change (a Hegelian dialectic) and, therefore, a
social science (economics) based upon timeless 'abstract' concepts was
destined rapidly to lose touch with social and economic reality. Neo-
classical economists rejected these criticisms, preferring to align their
discipline with those of the natural sciences to avoid contamination
by the doubtful integrity of the subjective, non-scientific social
sciences.

Summary

The academic domain that is known as 'business ethics' appears to have been an active area of enquiry for at least 100 years, with writers such as Ripley (cited in Carey, 1984); Niebuhr (1932); and Berle and Means (1932) making distinctive contributions in the first half of the twentieth century. Castro (1996) offers an interesting selection of readings on the historical trajectory of ethics in business.

The subject area developed with different orientations in different countries, even within the boundaries of western economies. The subject area in Germany and Scandinavian countries tended to have a focus upon the macro, systems level, whereas the American orientation appeared more obviously located at the individual level. The latter approach assumed that the economic system had a neutral effect upon business activity and its practitioners. Any acts or practices deemed unethical would therefore be the result of aberrant and/or unethical individuals. The UK position did not fit into either of these opposing positions, but possessed a much closer affinity with the American stance.

In De George's (1987) words:

> ... the easy work has ... been done ... the obvious problems have been raised and the obvious positions stated. Basic introductions have been written and anthologies assembled (p.206).

The demanding phase is yet to be adequately handled, that is the development of a coherent and consistent body of knowledge, evidence and argument that explains and assists in the development of ethical business practices and processes.

ENDNOTES:

---

[1] The Bubble Act of 1719 was a response to the South Sea Bubble scandal and had limited any form of partnership to 6 members. Its repeal in 1825 was judged necessary to broaden the financial base of companies whose financial needs were growing rapidly due to industrialisation. Although the limited liability company did not become law until 1855, "there is evidence to suggest that railway company directors [railway companies could be formed by Acts of Parliament] were manipulating reported profit and balance sheet data by the arbitrary treatment and classification of expenditure in order to stabilise dividends" (Lee and Parker, 1984). Acts of Parliament required records of accounts to be kept, *but not made available to the shareholders*. The Companies Clauses Consolidation Act of 1845 brought together all previous accounting provisions of other Acts and required that the balance sheet be audited, although there was no requirement for the auditor to be professionally qualified.

[2] This suggestion is made because with Higgs recommending that Boards of Directors should now be predominantly comprised of non-executive directors (and this being reflected in the 2003 Combined Code), the executive directors will meet as a group separate from the main board, creating a sort of two-tier board structure.

CHAPTER TWO

THE SIGNIFICANCE OF 'THE MARKET' WITHIN BUSINESS ETHICS DEBATES

Introduction

Cavanagh (1990) regarded the essential characteristics of American society, which in their most pristine economic form manifested themselves in market fundamentalism as the attachment to the 'frontier mentality', the primacy attaching to the 'individual' and the absolute commitment to maintain 'freedom' in its various forms. These concepts have been commented on, discussed and critically evaluated by many writers in their respective and different ways. Some have made their contributions in the role of advocate, (Baumol, 1975; Friedman, 1970; Hayek, 1944; Rand, 1999; and Spencer, 1857, 1862, 1892); while others have done so in the role of critic, (Bowles and Edwards, 1985, Galbraith, 1958; Lindblom, 1977; and MacIntyre, 1967). Some commentators cannot be easily located into either of these polar extremes, but have provided interesting analyses (Cavanagh, 1990; Glover, 2001; Held, 2002; Oakeshott, 1975; and Perri, 2002).

The advocates argue that any attempt to militate against the downside effects of economic Darwinism should be resisted strenuously. The essence of the arguments is exemplified in the writings of Ayn Rand[1] (Hull and Peikoff, 1999). Rand was born in Russia in 1905, but she emigrated to America when she was 21, nine years after the 1917 Bolshevik uprising in Russia, and four years after the end of the civil war that followed the uprising. On arriving in America Rand took a variety of low-paid, menial jobs. She is quoted as saying:

I had a difficult struggle, earning my living at odd jobs, until I could make a financial success of my writing. No one helped me, nor did I think at any time that it was anyone's duty to help me (cited in Fisher and Lovell, 2003, p.6).

Rand depicted man as:

... a heroic being, with his own happiness as the moral purpose of his life, with productive achievement as his noblest activity, and reason as his only attribute (cited in Fisher and Lovell, 2003, p.6).

Spencer (1857, 1862, 1892) was less concerned with romantic and heroic notions of the individual, but saw social, economic and political systems as bearing the hallmarks of biological systems, with increasing levels of differentiation and sophistication reflecting the survival of the fittest. Indeed, Spencer is actually credited with the development of this term and not Darwin. Turner (1985) argues that to be strictly accurate Spencer should not be called a social Darwinist, but that Darwin should be described as a Spencerian biologist.

Objectivism

Such snippets of historical context are helpful in understanding some of the factors that might explain an individual's philosophical position on key issues[2]. Randianism (the term used by followers of Rand) rejects government in anything other than its minimalist form, which is justified to protect individual rights, such as the police, the law courts and national defence forces. All other functions can, and should, be operated by 'the people', preferably *via* market mediation, and paid for (or not) by choice.

Rand is credited with developing the philosophical position that is known as objectivism. The pristine arguments of objectivism are the basis from which all variations of market-based economic-Darwinism trace their philosophical and argumentative roots. It is important to

rehearse these basic principles for they also form the context against
which counter arguments can be understood and judged.

(i) Reason is man's only means of knowledge. The facts of reality
     are only knowable through a process of objective reason that
     begins with sensory perception and follows the laws of logic.
     Objectivism rejects the existence of a God, because it lacks (to
     date) empirical support. However, in America, some of the most
     strident advocates of free-markets come from politically powerful
     religious groups. Thus, it should not be assumed that advocacy
     of the classical-liberal-economic approach is solely the province
     of atheists. Gottlieb (2001) and Ladd (1970) provide interesting
     reviews of the 'dream of reason', while Brockman (1995) reviews
     the increasing trend of scientists to communicate with the public
     at large, rather than to an exclusively academic audience (Dawkins,
     1988 and 2003; Rose and Rose, 2000). This trend of natural
     scientists to write in the popular press and publish 'non-academic'
     books on their subjects are seen as ways that the arguments of
     'reason' become accepted into the psyche of modern societies in
     subtle and discrete ways. The concern of critics (Rose and Rose,
     2000) is that the enlightenment view of reason as being able to,
     ultimately, provide all the answers to life, is being uncritically
     subsumed within people's psyche to such an extent that any theory
     purporting to be based upon 'reason' assumes ascendancy over less
     certain, less pedantic, more complex theories of human behaviour
     and human evolution.

(ii) Rational self-interest is the objective moral code. Objectivism
     rejects altruism (ie the greatest good is service to others) as an
     unhelpful and illogical human attribute. Man is required to pursue
     his own happiness, so long as it does not negatively affect anyone
     else's. This is compatible with Isaiah Berlin's (1999) negative
     freedom. This relates to a 'freedom-from' approach, where man

has a right to be free from interference by others, including, and in particular, government. As a concept, rational self-interest can be traced back through the work of writers such as, Bentham (1994; Burns and Hart, 1982); Hobbes (1998; Oakeshott, 1975; Peters, 1956); Hume (Flew, 1961; Ayer, 1981); Locke (1952, Dunn, 1984); Mill (Donner, 1991; Himmelfarb, 1974; Williams, 1976) and Smith (1759/1976). This trajectory of argument concerning human nature reflects the longevity of these debates, yet it is feared by some that the rational self-interest perspective is becoming too easily accepted within modern discourses, as exemplified by the Boeskyesque behaviour of many market operators in the late 1980s, and concerns over senior executives' remuneration packages of the 1990s and early 21st century (Solomon, 1992; Monks, 2003).

(iii) Laissez-faire capitalism is the objective social system. It is important to recognise that laissez-faire capitalism is referred to by its advocates as a social system, and not just an economic system. This is an important issue and one that critics of the approach feel unified in their opposition towards, although such opponents share differing views as to how to respond.

The need to minimise, preferably eliminate, institutional influence over corporate America is evident in the various legal statutes that have been passed in the United States. These laws have attempted to limit concentrations of power that might jeopardise market dynamics in particular areas, particularly the ability of financial institutions to exert influence over corporations *via* significant shareholdings. A possible unintended consequence of the protection afforded to corporate managers has been the development of, what is sometimes referred to as the Berle-Means corporation (Roe, 1994) where corporations are run by managers, for managers[3]. In the American model of corporate governance 'exit' is the preferred expression of shareholder disillusionment with inferior corporate performance. In the market for control, the 'voice' option, the influence by shareholders to change management behaviour, can be seen as undermining *managerial* sovereignty (Hirshman, 1996).

The major claims for the morality of 'the market', by its advocates, such as Friedman and Friedman (1962), Hayek (1960) and Joseph, (1976), are two-fold. The first is that the market is 'colour-blind and accent-deaf' (Crouch and Marquand, 1993), such that the market is unmoved by special situations. It is a pure meritocracy in that only those goods and services which possess the requisite characteristics of price, quality, and timing will survive in a competitive market. The consumer is the final arbiter between the competing claims of corporations on behalf of their products and the market is thereby an essential cornerstone of democratic societies. The second claim is that everybody, including the poor, will benefit from a general increase in economic growth – known as the trickle-down effect. It is not asserted that an overall increase in wealth will result in wealth differentials being lessened, or that a progression towards 'uniformity' or 'equality' will exist, but rather that the whole (social) scale will move upwards. The trickle-down effect is the enterprise culture's version of 'egalitarianism'. The fact that wide discrepancies exist in the quality of life of citizens subject to (imperfect) markets, and in many cases the quality of life has deteriorated from already desperate situations, are criticisms that market advocates feel able to defend on moral grounds. In response to the moral consequences of markets three explanations, or justifications, are proffered.

(1) As long as individual transactions are free of coercion and market outcomes are merely the aggregation of these individual decisions, then the process is procedurally just, or at least amoral.

(2) If the transactions are free of intentionally inequitable consequences then the (market) system cannot be criticised for what would be unintentional consequences. Injustice cannot be attributed to

unintentional outcomes and processes. For example, there might be unfavourable outcomes for some individuals (maybe even the majority of people), but these were not the intention of the market system. They are, thus, unintended consequences and therefore not subject to moral evaluation.

(3) Even if there was a moral case for criticising market-based outcomes, the lack of any agreed criteria for distributive justice severely undermines the criticism. Distributive criteria such as need, desert, justice, entitlement, rights, and contribution of effort, are not wholly compatible. Indeed, in some cases these are mutually exclusive. For example, someone who has been injured (not necessarily physically) as a result of a market-based transaction, which was unfairly skewed against that individual from the very beginning of the transaction, may nonetheless be totally unmoved by the loss because of their pre-existing wealth. Thus, whilst equity borne of justice might demand a re-distribution of societal resources to this individual, equity borne of need would offer a counter argument.

Negative freedom

Nozick (1974) also argued from the libertarian perspective, at least until the latter stages of his life. Nozick defended the libertarian position of negative freedoms, that is, the individual's right of 'freedoms from', as discussed above with respect to Ayn Rand. From a libertarian-market perspective, little outside the maintenance of property rights represented legitimate government activity. Differences in personal wealth, talent, physical attributes, and intelligence, were seen as 'natural' that owed nothing to social or political institutions and if legally obtained, then nothing could deny the owners their possession, or the value that derived from that ownership. Any differences in these qualities or characteristics did not justify the meddling of governments in attempting to re-distribute some of these benefits.

Within the libertarian frame of reference, as long as what individuals wished to do was within the law of the land, nothing should prevent individuals from fulfilling their desires. It is for this reason that taxation, and particularly the taxes levied on inherited assets, was such a vexed subject. From a libertarian perspective, taxation was the forcible, involuntary withdrawal of economic resources from individuals to be spent by governments in ways that might fail to satisfy, or be compatible with, the desires and values of the taxed individuals.

Nozick argued *via* 'entitlement theory' that what had been legally acquired could not be taken away within a libertarian concept of justice. This is despite the fact that practices that are regarded as immoral and illegal today, such as slavery, have not always been so, yet they represent an important factor in explaining the present distribution of wealth that shapes so many peoples' life-chances.

Nozick's entitlement theory attempted to draw a veil over the means by which wealth might have been acquired. The ramifications of being denied an equal opportunity to education, health care and legal justice were irrelevant within a libertarian conception of justice; a greater injustice would be to transfer 'legally' acquired assets from those that have to those that have not. With no limits attaching to what individuals could achieve in a liberal society, it was for every individual to improve their own life-chances, as per Randianism. This philosophy, with its economic, social and political implications, underpinned the rights, not just of individual citizens, but the entire economic infrastructure, particularly that of corporations. Corporations should be left unfettered by governmental fiat, to pursue their economic and business activities, with only the constraint of competition and 'market signals' to act as constraining or encouraging forces.

Thus, the relationship between waged labour and the owners of capital, was that the former were largely at the behest of the latter and that while the lives of individual citizens could not be predicted from this relationship, history and the principles of the relationship ensured that certain outcomes were predictable at the systems level. Individuals entered life in market-based economies with unequal attributes and characteristics. The system possessed inherently destabilising effects upon individual lives, even if these could not predict precisely which lives they would be (Turner and Trompenaars, 1993).

Distributive justice

A different approach to the issue of distributive justice was provided by Rawls (1971, 1999). Rawls treatise has had a significant impact upon debates associated with theories of justice and described 'the original position' as offering a reference point against which contemporary social, political and economic systems and conditions could be contrasted. Individuals and societies had to debate and decide what they wished to do about the differences between the "should be" and the "actual state" of the world. Hume (Ayer, 1981), had followed a tradition dating back to Aristotle, and located the source of justice within individuals, but Rawls' focused his attention upon institutions. It was these, Rawls argued, that would determine distributive justice, and maintain it. Hence, Rawls' emphasised the need to identify and establish mechanisms and institutions that would determine distributive justice at the time of the 'original position'.

The original position was an artifice of Rawls that allowed individuals to contemplate a 'just' society, without the burden of life experiences and prejudices tainting their views. Individuals envisaged a situation in which they had no knowledge of who they were, the political state in which they were born, or their economic, physical, ethnic and gender circumstances. Thus, the individual was placed behind what Rawls referred to as a 'veil of ignorance'. From this position of total ignorance the individual was then asked to make choices concerning the type of economic, social and political systems and institutions that they would choose. The 'just' society that emerged reflected Rawls' assumption that individuals were risk averse and would opt for structures, processes and laws that would support and protect the most vulnerable in society. This was specially true given the probability of being born into a developing economy with parents who existed on subsistence wages in a largely agrarian economy, with few national resources directed into health care and education, let alone an independent and just legal system. Rawls argued that the rational person would adopt a maximin, risk-averse, strategy that involved the study of all the worst-case scenarios that could exist within each choice. Having identified all the worst-case possibilities, the most preferred (maximum) options would then be selected.

Such an approach had the virtue of side-stepping the response that 'things are the way they are and one cannot change them'. Before any debate commenced on whether change was desirable, or even possible, an understanding of the nature of the problem, beyond the plaintive, that 'the system isn't fair' was required. It was essential that the forms of unfairness, and the institutions that would need to be in place to minimise, if not reduce, such unfairness were identified. The veil of ignorance was thus a mechanism by which the gaps between the actual and the desired could be established and debated.

Rawls' arguments were not without their critics, not least from those who argued that his theory of justice did not deal adequately with built-in injustices and inequities. For example, Pateman (1985) and Goodwin (1987) argued that Rawls dealt unsatisfactorily with the existing imbalances in power and authority. A significant criticism was that within Rawls' theory his 'difference principle' allowed and tolerated wide disparities in wealth, power and authority. Adopting a Pareto form of justification, great wealth and economic gains could be justified within Rawls' distributive justice, as long as the poorest in society were a little better off, or at the very least, no worse off as a result of a decision or business venture. Thus, Rawls was accused of developing a libertarian conception of justice, under a cloak of distributive justice, but one that possessed little effective distributive potential.

Within a market-based, competitive, capitalist system and free societies, the role of the market price was central, emerging, from the myriad of individual, independent and power-free transactions. Although prices may reflect these qualities there are some concerns that are far broader than this, particularly when environmental issues are brought into play. For market prices to reflect societal preferences the following factors have to exist:

a)   all the salient facts can be expressed in a numerical form;

b)   all the salient information, including that relating to the preferences of future generations has been articulated and allowed for, in the final 'market' price; and

c)   the 'right balance' of resource usage that places the resource in the hands of those who pay the highest price is the most appropriate 'solution'.

Summary

The market model has become the dominant mechanism for economic development in the developed world and from the neo-liberal position is the most ethical social system that allows individual preferences to emerge through market transactions and, as such, democracy is manifested through the market transactions rather than through the ballot box.

The ideas and arguments of Ayn Rand illuminated the neo-liberal view of market-based ethics, and the neutrality of market processes, that was a defence against criticisms of the skewedness of outcomes arising from market transactions. The conditions necessary for market prices to reflect the inclusive and democratic expression of societal preferences are further examined in chapters three and four.

ENDNOTES:

[1] Rand is reputed to be the favourite writer of Alan Greenspan who, at the time of writing, is the Chairman of the American Federal Reserve.

[2] Another interesting example is provided by Bauman (1994). He contrasts two philosophers, Knud Logstrup and Leon Shestov. Logstrup lived a tranquil and civilised life in Copenhagen. He wrote of human nature, "It is characteristic of human life that we mutually trust each other … . Only because of some special circumstance do we ever distrust a stranger in advance … initially we believe one another's word; initially we trust one another" (Bauman, 1994, p.1). Shestov, on the other hand, experienced great persecution during his life, under both the tsarist and anti-tsarist regimes and as a consequence had a far more pessimistic view of human nature, portraying the individual as one who is vulnerable and must at all times be ready to be betrayed. "In each of our neighbours we fear a wolf … we are so poor, so weak, so easily ruined and destroyed! How can we help being afraid?" Bauman, (1994, p.1).

[3] Cheffins (2001) initially disputes this assumption by reference to organisational developments in France, Spain, Germany and Italy, but later suggest that as globalisation takes hold the Berle-Means corporation will/has become the norm.

CHAPTER THREE

THE ROLE OF THE 'INDIVIDUAL' WITHIN BUSINESS ETHICS

Introduction

A major development in recent arguments concerning citizenship has been the re-conceptualisation of 'the individual' and this concept has changed, or been 'stretched' and now extends also to corporations. (The debate concerning the corporation as citizen is considered more fully in chapter eight.)

The American constitution was developed with the rights of the individual human citizen in mind (Tocqueville, 1946) but today the classical theories and debates concerning the individual in society possess a much wider relevance. Indeed some would argue that the 'rights' and sovereignty of the human individual are now threatened, and for some, superseded by the 'rights' of the corporation in modern society.

> *We originally sought to construct social institutions that would reflect our beliefs and our values; now there is a danger that our values reflect our institutions, that is organisations structure our lives to the point that we become locked in their grasp. We wind up doing certain things not because we choose to do them, but because that's how things are done in the world of organisations.* (Denhardt, 1981, p.322).

Neo-classical economics

The role and behaviour of the individual as consumer is central to neo-classical economics, however, although the neo-classical system is often described as a social system, and not just as an economic system, the view of the individual does not extend beyond that of a consumer. Marshall (1982) argued that the abstract nature of neo-classical economics meant that, even by the mid-19th century, it had become perceived by the German Historical School as:

> ... increasingly predisposed to attempt a statement of the corpus of economic life in an ever-decreasing number of theoretical propositions; falsely universal at the expense of the particular; excessively materialistic; wholly indifferent to the demands of 'culture' and its effects on the economic sphere; insufficiently historical; too much committed to laissez-faire and too dependent on a large number of empirically unverified assumptions about economic behaviour, notably that of the universal predominance of an income-maximising and self-interested 'rational economic actor'. (Marshall, 1982, p.26).

The criticism levelled at the Anglo–American attachment to neo-classical economics, and the role of the individual within the theory, was seen as deficient, or 'under-socialised' when considered from a sociological perspective. Employing the language of economics rather than sociology, the limitation of the neo-classical economics conception of the individual was that the wants of individuals were over-simplistically evaluated, using an unrealistically narrow set of decision variables. In essence, only "reason" was allowed to influence economic rationality. Emotions, values and circumstances did not feature in economic man's decision processes because to do so would introduce too many unpredictable variables into the decision-making model. The model would become enormously complex, to such an extent that its workability would be called into question, and predictability and generalisability, two fundamental conditions of the scientific method, would be lost.

The community

Etzioni (1988) observed that people had many wants, but once values were introduced into decisions, then these wants could easily be ordered, or regulated, by prices. Etzioni's approach provided a starting point that was fundamentally different from that of the neo-classical assumptions. In neo-classical economics, the individual was seen as being apart from society, but Etzioni's analysis recognised that the individual only effectively existed within a community, as part of, rather than apart from, society. Etzioni argued that being part of a community was central to people being able to approach acceptable levels of individuality. This was because being part of a community provided the bedrock for exercising individual choice and being free of "pressures from the authorities, demagogues, or the mass media" (1988). The idea that people rationally sought the most efficient means to their goals was replaced with a new decision-making framework that assumed that people typically chose largely on the basis of their emotions and value judgements, and only secondarily on the basis of logical and empirical considerations. These differences in the perspective and assumptions of these theories have profound implications for the issue of ethics in business.

Etzioni's arguments were anathema to free-marketeers. Etzioni's arguments attacked the sanctity of one of the cornerstones of free-market values that underpinned neo-classical economics, that of individual choice based on 'reason', and challenged the meaning of 'choice' inherent within the neo-classical notion of individualism. Etzioni was concerned that the 'individual' did not only exist as an isolated consumer.

However, 'community' did not equal a totalitarian uniformity in which individualism was lost or suffocated (Cavanagh, 1990). Drawing upon de Tocqueville, Cavanagh (1990) saw selfishness as a likely consequence of an increasing emphasis upon individualism. De Tocqueville argued that individualism might initially represent a "mature and calm feeling which disposes each member of the community to sever himself from the mass of his fellows and to draw apart with his family and his friends" (Cavanagh, 1990), but as individuals retreated to their own familiar turf they "leave society at large to itself" (p.42). De Tocqueville contrasted individualism and selfishness and found both to be 'seriously deficient'. As Cavanagh (1990) notes:

> *Selfishness originates in blind instinct: individualism proceeds from erroneous judgement more than from depraved feelings; it originates as much in deficiencies of the mind as in perversity of heart. Selfishness blights the germ of all virtue; individualism, at first, only saps the virtues of public life; but in the long run it attacks and destroys all others and is at length absorbed in downright selfishness.* (p.39).

Solomon (1993), however, asserted that individuals were who they were in the eyes of others, possessing qualities, characteristics, and personalities, only in as much as these traits were recognised by others. Therefore, 'others' gave, or confirmed a sense of self. These 'others' were the communities of which they were a part. Solomon's argument, drawn from an Aristotelian perspective, was that individualism did not exist in a vacuum, but was shaped by, and helped shape the contexts of life.

The new economy

Increasing attention has been given to the 'new economy' (Greenspan, 1998), where different writers have discussed the possibilities for, and the challenges to, ethical considerations from 'fast companies'. As Liedtka (2002) observes, economies are in a constant process of change and are, therefore, always 'new', and changes observable in the 1990s and progressing into the early years of the 21st century, suggest that fundamental shifts may be taking place that give a different resonance to the term 'new economy'. These changes relate primarily to developments in the flow, form and availability of information with associated ramifications for most forms of knowledge. The contributions of Brown and Duguid (2000); Evans and Wurster (2000); Kelly (1998); Shapiro and Varian (1999) and Stewart (1998) reflect the debate on these issues.

Other writers, (such as Handy, 1994) argued that the importance of the individual would increase in the new age of uncertainty, and that a feature of the new economy was that organisations would form very quickly to fill any information and/or commercial gaps, linking into, or creating free-forming, loose, networks of relationships. Companies within these networks might be relatively short-lived, as the information and commercial gap was gradually populated by other organisations. A number of the owners of the 'break-through' organisation would move on to fill another market gap, hence the 'fast' company tag. Such a vista offered the potential to individuals to create new opportunities resulting in a shift in power away from large, less flexible and less adaptive corporations (Liedtka, 2002). These new forms of organisations would be 'loose confederations of free agents, motivated by 'high-powered' incentives to pursue their own self-interests (Frank and Cook, 1995). Frank and Cook warned of the 'winner-takes-all mentality' that already existed in some fields but was accentuated by the 'fast-company'. Sennett (1998) expressed concern at the 'corrosion of character' that such dislocations from 'others' could breed. The advantages of agency were recognised, but Liedtka (2002) expressed concern at the moral toll that a loss of loyalty and long-term commitment could engender. In Sennett's view, the dull routine of Whyte's (1956), 'Organisation Man' trapped in the corporate bureaucracy, was exposed to less corrosiveness of individual character than today's 'freer-more-interesting-man', who was trapped in the productivity-obsessed firm. With the values of the new economy prioritising short-term performance and the environment being characterised by re-engineering, down-sizing, and cut-throat competition, loyalty became submerged by concerns for one's own survival, and only that.

To further support her concerns for the integrity of the 'self', Liedtka cites Kelly (1998):

> *Because the nature of the network economy seeds disequilibrium, fragmentation, uncertainty, churn and relativism, the anchors of meaning and value are in short supply. We are simply unable to deal with questions that cannot be answered by means of technology ... In the great vacuum of meaning, in the silence of unspoken values, in the vacancy of something large to stand for, something bigger than oneself, technology — for better or worse — will shape our society. Because values and meaning are scarce today, technology will make our decisions for us.* (p.6).

Sarason (1986), also focused upon the effect of modern conceptions of the individual and set his argument at the general level of concern about modern conceptions of individualism.

> *If **your** ethical dilemma is **your** responsibility according to **my** morality, this is quite consistent with the increasingly dominant ideology of individual rights, responsibility, choice and freedom. If **I** experience the issues as **yours**, it is because there is nothing in my existence to make it **ours**. And by ours I mean a social-cultural network and traditions which engender in members an obligation to be part of the problem and possible solution.* (p.87).

Poole (1991), however, offered a cautionary note to those calling for a recognition of the values inherent within a community-oriented paradigm, not so much because he had problems with the community ideal, but more in terms of its incompatibility with the dominant, modern portrayal of human activity, in all its various forms, increasingly reflecting a value-free notion of individualism. For Poole the problem was the unavailability of a sense of community:

> *The dominant forms of modern public life – the market, the capitalist organisation of production, the bureaucracy – are incomparable with community in this sense. Those who have invoked the concept against liberalism have simply evaded the central problem which liberalism is attempting to confront: the place of values in a value-free world.* (1991, p.88).

Recognising the tensions inherent within any debate that juxtaposes individualism and communitarianism, Etzioni (1988) argued for a different conception of individualism, that referred to a new relationship between the individual and society, between the individual and business, and between business and society. This conception was referred to as 'the I/We' perspective. By including both 'I' and 'We' in the decision frame, Etzioni argued that this represented a more realistic approximation to the tensions that infused any decision that touched many people, with all their varied, distinct and often conflicting needs and wants. A creative tension was acknowledged at the core of his theory, which involved a continuing search for a balance between the forces of individualism and that of the community of which individuals were a part:

> *As we see it individuals are neither simply depositories of their society's values nor free agents. They struggle to form their individual course, both building on and fending off the values their societies set, never free of them, yet never mere subjects. Similarly, on the macro or societal level, competition is beneficial as long as it is properly embedded in a supportive societal context, which ensures that the prerequisites of competition are met while limiting its scope … . …*

the I&We paradigm assumes that individuals experience perpetual
inner tension generated by conflicts among their basic urges (or desires),
among their various moral commitments, and between their urges and
their moral commitments. (Etzioni, 1988, pp.10/11).

Cultural spheres

Enderle (1995) and Walzer (1983) argued that societal life should
be seen as a series of spheres, which contained and constrained differing
elements of societal existence: the economic; the civic; the family; and
the state. In the economic sphere, markets were recognised as the most
effective mediating mechanism, and competition the most defensible
form of organisational coordination. Whilst markets, contracts and
competition were appropriate mediating elements, their relevance was
largely constrained within the economic sphere. Within the spheres
representing non-economic interpersonal relationships, were notions
of trust, care, welfare, sharing, friendship, leisure, and possibly even
altruism. There was some similarity between Walzer's analysis and
the work of Hegel (Singer, 1983), who also used a series of spheres to
conceptualise the social world.

McMylor (1994), also utilised the concept of spheres of activity
and commented upon the rise of the 'economic' relative to the other
spheres of social activity when he observed that:

The economic moved from being enmeshed within other dominating
frameworks to a situation in market societies when "the economy,
with a capital 'E' is no longer so embedded". The market means
that there is in some sense, a differentiation of economic activity
into a separate institutional sphere, no longer regulated by norms
that have their origin elsewhere. The individual economic agent is
free then to pursue economic self-interest, without 'non-economic'
hindrance. (p.100).

From a moral perspective, one of the problems with conceptualising the human world into separate spheres is that it may suggest that the spheres are independent to the point of allowing differing forms of behaviour to prevail within differing spheres, with behaviour being accepted, or at least tolerated, in one sphere that would not be acceptable in another. This is sometimes argued to be a recognition that people sometimes act in ways, when in 'business-mode', which they would not employ within their private, domestic lives. Walzer recognises this and argues that the spheres should not be seen as totally autonomous and independent. Rather he portrays a dynamic set of relationships between the spheres in which shifts between the spheres of particular facets of social life are inevitable. A sphere's scope and importance may wax and wane. Boundary conflict thus becomes endemic:

> *The principles appropriate to the different spheres are not harmonious with one another; nor are the patterns of conduct and feeling they generate. Welfare systems and markets, offices and families, schools and states are run on different principles: so they should be.* (Walzer, 1983, p.318).

However, Walzer goes on to argue that these principles must fit within a single culture. This is highly problematic, unless the single culture is one that recognises differences – and a multiplicity of cultures. Within such complexity wisdom becomes an important mediating factor, that is active and is always emerging through dialogue and debate such as in the Habermassian (1993) ideal where the dynamic of change is recognised, debated and progressed through a series of processes. However, these processes could be subject to 'social capture' by active groups and voices if participation was shirked by the general public. The Habermassian conception of "communicative action" demands an ideal level of public participation which when deviated from leaves scope for power imbalances to fill the void.

Altruism

An interesting contribution to the debate on individualism in modern society is that of altruism. Titmuss (1970), defended the altruism of individuals inherent in the donation of blood to the UK blood donor service. Titmuss was responding to calls for the UK service to operate as a commercial blood products clearing organisation, buying and selling blood, as in the United States.

> *In essence, these writers, … are making an economic case against a monopoly of altruism in blood and other human tissues. They wish to set people free from the conscience of obligation. Although their arguments are couched in the language of price elasticity and profit maximisation they have far-reaching implications for human values and all 'social service' institutions … . The moral issues that are raised extend beyond theories of pricing and the operations of the marketplace.* (Titmuss, 1970).

Titmuss worried about the wider implications of commercialising the blood donor service in the UK. If the altruism reflected in the voluntary and unpaid giving of blood was to be replaced by a commercial relationship, the sense of community inherent within the existing system would need to be replaced:

> *There is nothing permanent about the expression of reciprocity. If the bonds of community giving are broken the result is not a state of value neutralism. The vacuum is likely to be filled by hostility and social conflict, a consequence discussed in another context … the myth of maximising growth can supplant the growth of social relations.* (Titmuss, 1970).

Four economic and financial criteria were discussed by Titmuss, excluding the much wider and unquantifiable social, ethical and philosophical aspects to concentrate upon those aspects that economists would recognise. These were: (i) economic efficiency; (ii) administrative efficiency; (iii) price – the cost per unit to the patient; and (iv) purity, potency and safety, or the quality per unit.

> *On all four criteria the commercialised blood market fails. However, paradoxically … the more commercialised a blood distribution system becomes (and hence more wasteful, inefficient and dangerous) the more will the GNP be inflated. In part, … this is the consequence of statistically 'transferring' an unpaid service (voluntary blood donors, voluntary workers in the service, unpaid time) with much lower external costs to a monetary and measurable paid activity involving costlier externalities.* (Titmuss, 1970, p.205).

Plant (1992), questioned whether markets were the most appropriate mediating mechanism for medical services, and explored the possibilities for a free-market in body parts (human organs) in general, as well as the justification for a market-based ethos replacing a service ethic in non-voluntary, public service organisations. With regard to a market for human body parts Plant (1992) observed that:

> *On a strictly capitalist view of market principles, it is very difficult to see why there should not be such a market. The scope for a market is clearly quite wide. There could be a market in blood and blood products; in kidneys; in sperm; in renting out a uterus for surrogate pregnancy; and so forth.* (p.91).

Plant argued that from a market perspective, at least three principles would favour a market in these areas:

(1) there was a clear demand;

(2) the current donor system was failing to meet demand; and

(3) ownership of human organs was clear and would not be undertaken by the donor if it was not in their personal interest.

Despite strong advocacy for such markets, broad public support was (and appears to continue to be) lacking. Plant argued that this reluctance reflected a form of boundary being drawn by society, with human organs currently residing outside the boundary that defined the limit of market application.

These concerns are important because the more an individual feels isolated and impotent, the more the business community becomes immune from a collective social opposition to practices that reflect contentious and problematic ethics. This scepticism over the degree of individualism that actually existed within neo-classical views of 'the individual' was shared by Nisbet (1953):

> *The politics of enslavement of man requires the emancipation of man from all the authorities and memberships ... that serve, one degree or another, to insulate the individual from the external political power ... totalitarian domination of the individual will is not a mysterious process, not a form of sorcery based upon some vast and unknowable irrationalism. It arises and proceeds rationally and relentlessly through the creation of new functions, statuses and allegiances which, by conferring community, makes the manipulation of the human will scarcely more than an exercise in scientific, social psychology ... there maybe left the appearance of individual freedom, provided it is only individual freedom. All of this is unimportant, always subject to guidance and control, if the primary social contexts of belief and opinion are properly organised and managed. What is central is the creation of a network of functions and loyalties reaching down into the most intimate recesses of human life where ideas and beliefs will germinate and develop. (pp.202 and 208).*

Utopian ideals

The business ethics debate can also take an idealistic direction. For example, the "ideal speech act" may be a utopian position that possesses little practical relevance. In defence of utopian benchmarks, Cavanagh (1990) referred to Mannheim (1936) with reference to the loss to human meaning if utopia were dismissed from society's vocabulary, where a society's understanding, and ability to comprehend what might be possible would be diminished. Mannheim used the term 'utopia' to describe any conception that possessed elements that went beyond reality. This was not as extreme as Thomas More's *Utopia* (1516), that meant the idealistic concept of perfection, but rather a benchmark that represented a state beyond that which currently obtained, but which might be possible if current assumptions, values and/or beliefs could be changed. The risks associated with denying any conceptions of human possibilities beyond those which currently obtained concerned Bloom (1987) (quoted in Cavanagh, 1990, p.250) who referred to such a closing of minds as follows:

> *Minds are like parachutes, they only work when they are open ...*
> *all great civilizations were steeped in knowledge of other times and*
> *other thinkers. But American universities have virtually stopped*
> *conveying a tradition. Since we so rarely examine the most important*
> *questions (eg what is a good life), we have become a pragmatic,*
> *shallow civilisation.*

Ethical schizophrenia

The existence of different values underpinning business ethics was referred to by Chewning (1984) as ethical schizophrenia. Chewning expressed concern that different levels of morality might become acceptable in different spheres of social activity, particularly between the values and ethics of the family and citizenship and that of business life. He argued that ethical schizophrenia would lead, in the longer term, to a gradual infusion of economic values into the other spheres. The migration of the values embedded in the economic sphere into the other spheres was a prospect, or possible reality, that Walzer warned against:

> *One can conceive of the market as a sphere without boundaries, an unzoned city – for money is insidious, and market relations are expansive. A radically laissez-faire economy would be like a totalitarian state, invading every other sphere, dominating every other distributive process. It would transform every social good into a commodity. This is market imperialism.* (pp.119-120).

An example of business values being migrated to the family sphere is the marriage contract. Marriage rituals symbolise a commitment from one human being to another and whilst the legal rules relating to ownership of a married couple's assets have changed through time, the commitment has ostensibly been for life. A contract employed within marriage has traditionally taken the form of a social contract, with the concepts, or virtues, of love, care, trust, justice and duty being essential elements of that contract. Increasingly, however, the form of contract has moved from an unwritten, social understanding to one represented by a formal document, with the division of a couple's assets, in the event of the couple divorcing, being articulated in a legally binding pre-nuptial agreement. In America at least, legally enforceable marital contracts are formally replacing the social contract.

This example illustrates how the cementing of a relationship, once so fundamentally different between business and social practice, has now come much closer together. As trust within business relationships diminished through time, so business agreements were increasingly articulated in written contracts. Interestingly, the most important parts of contemporary business contracts are often not those aspects that are intended to bind the respective parties to the deal, but rather the clauses that stipulate the penalties of breaking the contract, for contract-breaking is seen as an increasingly likely outcome. The trust necessary to keep a legally enforceable contract working has been undermined and hence has become an unreliable basis of many relationships. Pre-nuptial agreements can be interpreted as an increasing loss of trust in personal relationships. Ironically, with business organisations so committed to achieving heightened levels of efficiency and economy, it is paradoxical that such vast sums of money are spent on the entire legal, pre-contract and post-contract, monitoring and auditing paraphernalia, when trust, if it was respected and engrained, would be so much more economic, efficient, effective and civilised.

Summary

The individual is a lauded and central element to libertarian conceptions of a free society, but is only allowed a stunted and limited role within libertarian economics as a consumer. The unfettered, unconstrained life of the individual, is a key requirement of libertarian economics because the same principles underpin the assumptions of business activity. Yet the interests and demands of business and the individual are not always compatible. Indeed the interests of the individual can sometimes only be nurtured at the expense of the other. The concern is that the commodification of man will become a reality if the economic sphere is allowed to engulf the other spheres of human activity, particularly if the values and virtues of the enlarging economic sphere are seen to be justifiably different from those that underpin the other, 'waning' spheres. Possibly the most contentious issue is that raised by Caputo (1993) and Poole (1991), that questions how individuals engage in and stimulate debate values in societies that are increasingly encouraged to be reason-ladened, but value-free.

CHAPTER FOUR

THE SIGNIFICANCE OF VALUES AND VIRTUES WITHIN BUSINESS ETHICS DEBATES

Introduction

The issue of values and virtues is central to any discussion of business ethics. Spaemann (1989) discusses the way that the Greeks strove to understand 'the object of our basic and fundamental wants' to distinguish between those codes or behaviours that were natural, and helped human beings achieve what they fundamentally wanted, or unnatural and oppressive. This orientation towards thinking rigorously about the meaning of life has some bearing on those people who operate in business in ways with which they are uncomfortable. They feel unable to change their situation and become the *potential* whistleblower but 'how many people, who find themselves in an uncomfortable business situation would turn the situation into a philosophical problem'? (Lovell, 2002; Miceli and Near, 1992). Spaemann (1989) argues that this is not just a development of the atomisation of the individual, but also a diminution of the spiritual and philosophical part of man's intellectual tool kit. Spaeman (1989) picks up Bauman's (1994) point concerning the organisational (ethical) boundaries within which individuals are required to act, separating those activities which are organisationally focused and, thus, not a subject for ethical concern, from 'other', presumably non-organisationally focused, and thus moral issues. Baumol (1975) argued that business activity was neither moral nor immoral, but rather amoral. That is, business life was subject to a different set of values and relationships, and that business actions had to be judged by 'the business case', not by a business-free, socially determined ethics of practice.

Business as amoral

De George (1982) addressed morality as something that people acted on in their private lives, but in business these personal feelings were put aside because of the amorality of business. He argued that while the 'frontier spirit' of early 'Business America' had served the country 'magnificently' in delivering a rich variety of goods, at as low a price as possible, and in so doing had provided employment and helped society as a whole achieve the good life, the business mandate had since changed. The relationship was now far more symbiotic and sensitive. A frontier spirit was no longer appropriate.

Since De George published his article in 1982 the era of Ivan Boesky and Michael Milkin in the late 1980s has come and gone, but in the early years of the 21st century acceptance of the changing business mandate that De George spoke of is, at best, a contested, problematic observation, such as: the issue of directors' remuneration packages; the looming pensions crisis in the UK and Continental Europe; and multiple charges of unethical practices by corporations in baby food products, pharmaceutical, timber, oil and other mineral extraction industries.

From a libertarian perspective the centrality of freedom to any discussions concerning agency and rights is unimpeachable. It is an evocative symbol that harks back to the frontier spirit of early, modern America. However, the conception of freedom as articulated by politicians and neo-classical economists is often too simplistic and superficial. This complex concept is capable of more refined analytical treatment, as evidenced by writers such as Berlin (1969); Gray (1989);

Hobbes (1968); MacIntyre (1977 and 1981); Mill (1971 and 1998); Oakeshott (1962 and 1983); and Rawls (1971).

Freedom

Berlin (1969) categorised freedom into two forms; negative freedoms and positive freedoms. The latter relates to 'freedoms to' make choices and to partake in actions purely of one's own volition. Negative freedoms are 'freedoms from', predominantly government intervention or diktat in one's private life. There is a tension within libertarian thinking with regard to positive freedoms. If positive freedom is the fundamental right of all citizens to make independent choices, then the implicit egalitarian orientation within positive freedom, at least with respect to the distribution of power, is challenged by the prevailing unequal distribution of economic power. Economic power is an increasingly dominant form of power, in some ways more so than political power because it is often less visible, or at least more elusive, but, nonetheless, 'pulling the strings of political power'. With such a high proportion of populations lacking economic power, and with corporations increasingly assuming the mantle of *citizens, economic power becomes a disturbing and complicating element in debates about freedom* (Held, 1987).

Hayek (1960, 1973 and 1976), a leading defender of market systems and libertarian philosophy, was not an advocate of democracy, and saw it as a creed that had the potential to destroy both capitalism and democracy itself (Hayek, 1973). While libertarian economists claimed that economics should be 'value-free', economic theory had at its bedrock certain assumptions, beliefs and values and liberal neo-classical economics was no exception. However, Hayek's values were more complex than other libertarian economists (Dunleavy and O'Leary, 1987) and placed liberty at the centre of his economic philosophy, with markets acting as discovery mechanisms placing the maximisation of knowledge and its efficient transfer above that of liberty. This complicated Hayek's apparent opposition to democracy, because a robust commitment to knowledge and its availability supports democratic principles.

Bellah *et al.* (1985) argued that negative freedom failed to address the interdependence of individuals in modern, complex urban society.

> *Freedom is perhaps the most resonant, deeply held American value. In some ways, it defines the good in both personal and political life. Yet freedom turns out to mean being left alone by others, not having other people's values, ideas or styles forced upon one, being free of arbitrary authority in work, family and life. What it is that one might do with that freedom is much more difficult for Americans to define. And if the entire social world is made up of individuals, each endowed with the right to be free of others' demands, it becomes hard to forge bonds of attachment to, or cooperation with, other people, since such bonds would imply obligations that necessarily impinge on one's freedom.* (p.23).

The resistance to government intervention in human activities transferred through to the activities of corporations. Cheffins (2001) compared the extent to which corporate actions in America and the UK were subject to either government constraint or interference by financial institutions. Cheffins contrasted the slightly different routes that the US and the UK had taken in arriving at relatively similar stances with regard to managerial sovereignty. It is somewhat ironic that although Berle and Means' concerns about the dislocation of ownership and control was published in 1932, all the subsequent initiatives to protect the efficient working of 'the market' and the sovereignty, or the rights, of the individual corporation to operate free of government and institutional constraints, accentuated agency issues and resulted in shareholder interests being achieved in only indirect ways, and sometimes, not at all. Thus, an unintended consequence has been to raise management sovereignty above that of shareholder sovereignty.

Legislation has been passed on a number of occasions in the United States to address the concentration of financial power, such as anti-trust legislation. Whilst this legislation has been concerned with more than financial institutions, the minimisation of the concentration of financial power has been a constant issue in the US.

> … the Berle-Means Corp. was an adaptation that arose to fit the kind of financial system produced by regulatory intervention. (Cheffins, 2001, pp.101-102).

An emphasis upon freedom as a central attribute of American society is recognised by Bellah et al. (1985) as a virtue, but one that possesses negative aspects that are too often ignored when discussions of capitalism and markets take place:

> Making freedom such an important value has given Americans a respect for other individuals and has encouraged creativity and innovation. However, it also has its costs. … It is an ideal freedom that leaves Americans with a stubborn fear of acknowledging structures of power and independence in a technologically complex society dominated by giant corporations and an increasingly powerful state. The state of freedom makes Americans nostalgic for their past, but provides few resources for talking about their collective future … . As people live closer together and become more dependent upon one another, freedom must be constrained by both self-control and external checks. In fact, real freedom paradoxically emerges only when a people have formed internal constraints. (pp.23-24).

The paradox of freedom, referred to by Bellah et al. (1985), was also recognised by Viereck (1953) when he observed that:

Freedom is endangered if a free society's shared values are no longer sufficiently vigorous to preserve the moral cohesion on which the discipline of free people rests. (p.196).

However, the need for self-reflection was, for Schlesinger (cited by Cavanagh, 1990), reflected in the American antipathy towards considering issues of ideology and philosophy and jeopardising an innovative and entrepreneurial people (see also Kristol, 1973). Schlesinger argued that most Americans would not allow ideology to contaminate their attachment to experience and possibly narrow their 'spectrum of choice', and this, Schlesinger argued, was probably the most important and positive attribute the early settlers brought to America. Cavanagh (1990) asserted that this basic American approach was part of the attitude that encouraged innovation and experiment that was part of the dominant empirical and pragmatic American way of life.

One of the problems with such an unflinching attachment to individual freedom is that it manifests itself in social and economic Darwinism. Organisational activity is judged to be equivalent to individual activity and the purity of both has to be protected by negative freedoms. Intervention by institutions of authority (political or otherwise), is regarded by economic fundamentalists as unacceptable, because it undermines freedom of choice and saps the integrity of the mythologised 'individual'. Even if 'natural' corrections to market 'problems' take time, this is judged to be infinitely preferable, notwithstanding the human suffering that this entails, to government or institutional intervention. This economic Darwinist approach favours corporate governance initiatives that are voluntary; where 'exit' is the preferred shareholder response to corporate underperformance rather than a 'voice' strategy.

Greed

Such a context was discussed by Solomon (1992) when he reflected upon the greed events that took place on the 41st floor of Salomon Brothers in the late 1980s. He expressed concern at the sight of "recently graduated MBAs making hundreds of thousands, or even millions of dollars employing other people's money". Solomon was concerned with bringing integrity into business not to dismantle business:

> *Business ... is as old as civilisation itself,* [and] *is an essential part of our culture ... because it depends upon and presupposes the virtues and that basic sense of community and mutual trust without which no activities of production or exchange or mutual benefit would be possible.* (p.17).

He lamented upon the trend of treating financial markets as if they were casinos:

> *.... Business life is reduced to the thrill of the market and its 'lottery winnings'. There is no pride in one's products (they are just new and better instruments for making money), no sense of dignity or 'service' in one's services.* (p.17).

What affronted Solomon was that business was portrayed as a game, whereas he saw it as part of a community of others. Acting with integrity might not always prove profitable but that was part of the ebb and flow of product life cycles and of business life.

Solomon (1992) refuted *homo economicus* because it characterised man as only a financial utility maximiser. For *homo economicus,* making money became an end in itself. This dislocation reflected the lack of identity, or understanding, that people had with products or services that were beneficial to others and in which they could take a personal pride:

The making of money pure and simple is not the culmination of business life, much less the fulfilment of one's social responsibilities. The very way we think about business has somehow gone very wrong, not just in its details [eg the Salomon example] but at its very conception. (pp.18–19).

Mahoney (1990) echoed Solomon's concerns about the dislocation of business activity from a sense of service, although unlike Solomon, Mahoney's analysis drew upon religious and theological arguments. Mahoney argued that material success was not sought for its own sake, but:

… as evidence of divine approval of one being numbered among the 'elect' whom alone an inscrutable God was saving from eternal damnation. … In due course such ingrained character traits of self-reliant individualism and of strong personal elitism became free-standing, divorced from their theological and religious foundation, and they found a congenial secular rationale not only in the American 'frontier spirit', but also in the nineteenth-century theory of Social Darwinism (Klein, 1985). *Thus, the worst features of aggressive individualism were to find justification in the view that not only is survival of the fittest in any society a matter of historical record; it is also a prerequisite for individual and social progress.* (p.9).

Mahoney developed his argument by discussing the 'cult of the individual' in American society. Citing Bellah *et al.* (1985) Mahoney saw the fixation upon 'the star' as reflective of a fundamental tension in American life and values:

The American dream is often a very private dream of being the star, the uniquely successful and admirable one, the one who stands out from the crowd of ordinary folk who don't know how. And since we have believed in that dream for a long time and worked very hard to make it come true, it is hard for us to give it up, even though it contradicts another dream that we have – that of living in a society that would really be worth living in. (Mahoney, 1990, p.8).

Virtue

Virtue, and what is virtuous draws upon Aristotle (1976), who developed the ideas of his teacher, Plato. Plato identified four principle virtues: those of wisdom; courage; self-control; and justice. Aristotle added a number of other virtues to Plato's, including patience, truthfulness and magnificence. However, in Aristotle's Greece and particularly the city state of Athens, the virtues only applied to the male elite. Athens, at that time, was a stable city-state, but also class-ridden. For the elite it was a civilised, culturally rich environment, in which much time could be given to contemplating and debating philosophical issues in public and private. However, four hundred years before Aristotle's birth, in the time of Homer, Greece was subject to constant hostilities and the virtues then were those of a great warrior not the noble citizen or philosopher. Other periods of time have also reflected these changing societal values (MacIntyre, 1967). With the rise of Christianity, new values began to assume prominence. For example, the New Testament presented an image of 'goodness' that was unlikely to be obtainable to the wealthy and the privileged, if the acquisition of wealth and power were their only claims to goodness. Only the poorest were deemed worthy in the New Testament, where a slave, the lowest of society in Aristotle's Athens, was more deserving and, thus, more worthy than a rich man.

The frugality of a Puritan existence carried on the New Testament's beliefs of attaching little value to material possessions, but Protestantism, and its Puritan form, was far more accommodating to business dealings than the Catholic Church, particularly with respect to the principle of usury. The prohibition of usury, as defined by the scriptures, gradually became increasingly unpopular and when Jean

Calvin decreed, in the early sixteenth century, the practice inappropriate for a mercantile society, the dominance of commercial values began to take hold (Buckley, 1998; and Tawney, 1966).

This development was reflected in the pronouncements of Benjamin Franklin (1996/1785), who enumerated thirteen virtues, which included 'justice', 'humility' and 'moderation', that were Aristotelian in character, and also ranked the virtues of 'silence', industry' and 'cleanliness', which were all work orientated attributes. Similarly, both David Hume (Ayer, 1981) and Adam Smith (Rae, 1895; Raphael and Macfie, 1976; Smith, 1759/1976 and 1776/1976) wrote of the virtues that commerce and manufacturing enhanced or brought into the world. These were industriousness, assiduity, frugality, punctuality and probity. The latter was highlighted by Hirshman (1996) as extremely important for the functioning of a market society.

By Franklin's time the needs of industry and commerce had become essential characteristics of contemporary life and not just of economic life. This was a long way removed from virtue in Aristotle's time when work was regarded as demeaning, something to be undertaken by slaves and other underlings. Athenian citizens owned property or businesses, but *work* within these organisations was undertaken by other, lesser members of society. The social relationships within Aristotle's Athens possessed some of the characteristics of both feudal and capitalist societies, although the interests of the Athenian citizen were directed towards philosophical and artistic endeavours in more direct ways than is normally associated with feudal and capitalist societies.

In Aristotelian terms, a virtuous life was one that allowed man to achieve his *telos,* or end, to its full potential. Practice of the virtues made this potential realisable. The emphasis was thus upon both means (virtues) and ends (*telos*). In The New Testament, and those of the other major religions, the virtues (the means) prepare the believer for what is to follow (the *telos*). From these perspectives, the means must possess integrity and respect notions of justice in order that the ends retain their purity. Within these debates, dubious means tarnish and jeopardise desired ends.

In Franklinian terms, virtue was dependent upon utility, productivity and efficiency. As a result, the achievement of accepted societal ends, which by the mid-eighteenth century were expressed predominantly in material terms, could justify less than virtuous means. The 'end' was a worldly one, although the religious underpinning of American life squared the difficult circle that the Puritan attachment to frugality had posed, by deeming that those who achieved material wealth were the 'chosen' ones as they were rewarded in this life as well as the one to come, because of their 'particular' qualities (Mahoney, 1990). Worldly ends, such as enhanced efficiency, could be used to justify less than defensible means, such as unsafe or unhealthy working practices, or the exploitation of vulnerable groups.

A further example of the changing notion of virtues, was in the use of the concept of self-interest, or as it was referred to in the eighteenth century, self-love. Hirsch (1977) used Levitt (1956) as an example of those who interpreted and lauded self-love/self-interest as selfishness:

> *What is important is that the pursuit of self-interest has become institutionalised … this is of the greatest importance for the future of capitalism.* (Levitt, 1956, cited in Hirsch, 1977, p.137).

In both *The Theory of Moral Sentiments* (1759, although the sixth edition and most revised version was published in 1790), and *The Wealth of Nations* (1776), Smith referred to the role of self-interest (self-love) as central to an understanding of human nature and human behaviour within an economic system. Buckle (1861) criticised Smith for being inconsistent in the values within the two treatises.

Werhane (2002) takes exception to the fact that "almost since his death there has developed a caricature of … *The Wealth of*

Nations" (Werhane, 2002), and argued that Smith did not promulgate a Hobbesian notion of egoistic human motivation. While Smith referred to the natural liberty of man to pursue his own interests, where "all systems ... of restraint, therefore, being thus completely taken away" (Smith, 1759/1976), a critical element to Smith's analysis and prognosis is invariably overlooked. Latter-day interpretations of Smith's arguments ignore that it was not just the force of the idealised perfect and free market that allowed some form of ethical, as well as economic, equilibrium to prevail, but also the underlying morals and ethics that supported Smith's analysis. A detachment of the latter from the former leaves a vacuum that is filled (á la Titmuss) with distorted levels of self-interest that are unconstrained by moral imperatives and transcend into myopic self-centeredness and selfishness.

With regard to action, Smith recognised a variety of motives, not only for action in general but also for virtuous action. Among these motives Smith included self-interest. However, Smith's notion of self-interest was quite different from selfishness and Smith made a clear distinction between the two, identifying the latter with harm and neglect of other people. Hirsh (1977) cites Coates (1971) to illustrate the relationship between the social values implicit within *The Theory of Moral Sentiments* and the economic values of *The Wealth of Nations*:

> [Men] *could safely be trusted to pursue their own self-interest without undue harm to the community not only because of the restrictions imposed by the law, but also because they were subject to built-in restraint derived from morals, religion, custom and education.* (Coates, 1971, p.9).

In a similar vein, John Stuart Mill (1970/1848) expressed appal at the prospect of a market led society:

> *The idea is essentially repulsive of a society held together only by the relations and feelings arising out of pecuniary interests.*

The cultural cement of moral and religious values would be weakened by the corruption of self-interest or the contemporary notion of self-love.

Within the Franklinian conception of virtues are the seeds of what troubles many regarding the juxtaposition of ethics and business. Some of the virtues articulated by Franklin can be achieved most effectively by the suppression of individual rights, such as silence and industry, whilst others, such as punctuality and cleanliness, are virtues, not primarily because they benefit the individual concerned, but because they contribute to the economy and efficiency of business. Thus, whilst the ends (punctuality and cleanliness) can be regarded as beneficial in themselves, they would not be regarded as virtues from an Aristotelian perspective, because they are driven by a concern with others' ends, not the individual concerned, and the means are of little consequence, other than their support for the broader end. One of the problems with this instrumentality is that it turns people exclusively into "means" and lays capitalism open to the Marxist critique of the exploitation and ultimate feelings of anomie experienced by the individual. Schumpeter (1976) sees the seeds of capitalism's ultimate demise in the manifestations of its own success:

> We have … seen that it [capitalism] *tends to wear away protective strata, to break down its own defenses, to disperse the garrisons of its entrenchments.* … *capitalism creates a critical frame of mind which, after having destroyed the moral authority of so many other institutions, in the end turns against its own; the bourgeois finds to his amazement that the rationalist attitude does not stop at the credentials of kings and popes but goes on to attack private property and the whole scheme of bourgeois values.* (Schumpeter, 1976, quoted in Cavanagh, 1990, p.116).

Weber saw rationalism, and not capitalism, as the central problem facing Western societies, because the latter was merely a significant manifestation of rationalism with the further logical consequence of commercial development of globalisation.

Summary

This chapter has explored the concepts of freedom and liberty. For many, the tensions inherent with simplistic calls for 'more freedom' and 'less government' demand examination. For example, Bellah *et al.* (1985) argue that demands for less government fail to address the interdependence of individuals in modern, complex, urban societies. Viereck (1953) challenged the neo-liberal advocates to accept that freedom is endangered if a free society's shared values are no longer sufficiently vigorous to preserve the moral cohesion on which the discipline of free people rests.

The problems of the values of the economic sphere coming to dominate the other spheres of human activity (Walzer, 1983) was explored through the ideas and arguments of writers such as Solomon (1992) and Mill (1970/1848). For Solomon, "the making of money pure and simple is not the culmination of business life, much less the fulfilment of one's social responsibilities". The very way we think about business has somehow gone very wrong, not just in its details [*eg* the Solomon example] but at its very conception (Solomon, 1992). For Mill (1970/1848), "the idea is essentially repulsive of a society held together only by the relations and feelings arising out of pecuniary interests".

However, for Weber, the central problem was not so much with capitalism, but reason which manifested itself in neo-classical economic theory in the form of rational economic man and the values that drove such an actor. Weber was profoundly concerned and distressed at the paradox that it was "both the highest achievement of the West and the source of the 'soullessness' of contemporary life". (Hughes, 1979).

Reason has come to challenge and increasingly supplant religious values and beliefs, and these elements of the 'ethics in business' debate are now examined in chapter five.

CHAPTER FIVE

RELIGIOUS VALUES AND PRINCIPLES IN THE BUSINESS ETHICS DEBATE

Coates (1971) identified the influence of morals, religion, custom and education as important in understanding the factors at play in the mid-late eighteenth century that allowed self-love to be a wholly compatible trait with business activity, together with respect for others both individually and collectively. For Adam Smith self-interest, or self-love, was a wholly different concept to selfishness. While Adam Smith is invariably associated with *The Wealth of Nations*, too often his other major treatise *The Theory of Moral Sentiments* is overlooked, yet one treatise informs the other. Smith, although regarded as a central figure in classical economics, was in fact appointed to the Chair of Moral Philosophy at the University of Glasgow in 1752, having already been appointed to the Chair of Logic the year before. *The Theory of Moral Sentiments* was first published seventeen years before *The Wealth of Nations,* and informed and underpinned Smith's thinking and arguments about the nature of business relationships. It was a profound sense of morals that prevented self-interest being confused with, or becoming, selfishness.

Attempts have been evident in recent years to reassert, or realign, the ethical base of business with religious values and principles (Abeng, 1997; Alhabshi and Ghazali, 1997; Boatright and Naughton (2002); Childs, 1997; Cortright and Naughton, 2002; Dorff, 1997; Epstein, 2002; Goodpaster, 2000 and 2002; Green, 1997; Jeremy (1990); Levine, 1987; Lodge (1982); Nelson, 1949; Noonan, 1957; Schnall, 1993; and Tamari, 1987). Goodpaster (2002) identified three factors that had emerged during a period of self-reflection and critical probing of free-market capitalism since the Second World War, and particularly during the past twenty-five years. These were:

1. The modern business corporation needed a *raison d'être* that went beyond compliance with competitive forces and government regulation. Those leading businesses had to inculcate an internally determined and agreed understanding of the corporation's relationships. This was not necessarily stakeholding, but it did not exclude it.

2. The decisive factor of production was knowledge and organised information and this placed a premium upon individuals, and those who possessed key knowledge and associated skills, but marginalised and alienated larger numbers of employees; and

3. The phenomenon known as globalisation and its "implicit transcendence of national and cultural boundaries, called for an ethical platform rooted not in legal jurisdictions or international conventions, but in a shared human concern for justice and the common good" (Goodpaster, 2002).

The third observation came from a collection of essays that focused upon a rethinking of business's purpose, and concern for the corporate moral malaise and reflected a 'Catholic social tradition' (Cortright and Naughton, 2002). Clearly this could raise the accusation of religious imperialism, unless the intent was purely ecumenical, or the essays were offered as a contribution to a debate in which all the theological positions were being encouraged to participate.

Other writers have also addressed business ethics from specific religious perspectives. For example, Abeng (1997); Alhabshi and Ghazali (1997); and Baydoun and Willett (2000) offer Islamic perspectives on particular facets of contemporary business issues, while Dorff (1997); Green (1997); Levine (1987) and Schnall (1993) have done so from a

Jewish perspective. The Christian perspective has been represented by writers such as Calkins (2000); Calvez and Naughton (2002); Orwig (2002); and Nash and McLennan (2001). Whilst publications on Sikhism do not refer directly to business issues, the underpinning values are compatible with those of a business element within society that is founded upon integrity and honesty (Singh, 1992). Interestingly the father of the first Sikh guru, Guru Nanak, was described as a village accountant (Singh, 1992).

Other writers have addressed the specific business issue, of usury from different religious perspectives (*eg* Noonan, 1957; Nelson, 1949). Interestingly, while Islam maintains a commitment to not recognising usury, the Christian religions had accepted usury in general transactions by the fifteenth century, recognising the growing significance of trade and commerce and the associated power and influence of the mercantile class.

An interesting difference between Islam and Christian religions is the theoretical position of wealth and property. While Lutheran and early Calvinist approaches lauded hard work, thrift and dedication, later Calvinism introduced 'signs of election' (Green, 2002), or worldly signs that one had been identified by God as one of the 'chosen' and as a result had been allowed significant worldly goods. This rationalisation of wealth disparities ultimately manifested itself in economic success being seen as a sign of blessedness, and poverty associated with moral and spiritual failure, especially with regard to an unwillingness to work (Green, 2002). Within Islam, however, the principle of vicegerency placed the owner of property in the position of tenant or agent, holding the goods or property in trust on behalf of God. In theory this placed the environment in a more protected position than was the theoretical position within the Christian tradition, and closer to the Heideggerian position discussed later in chapter seven.

A feature which links many of the major religions is the experiences of the religious leaders with respect to business affairs. The

Prophet Mohammed[1] was forced to depart to Medina from Mecca as a consequence of his growing outspokenness against the greed and materialism he saw in Mecca (Ling, 1968); Jesus was disgusted at the money lenders in the Temple and the attachment to material possessions (eg Matthew (6: 19, 24; 20-23; 21: 12-13); Mark 10: 23-25; 11:15) and Luke 12: 16-21; 17: 28-30; 18: 22-25 19:45-46); Gautama's (the Buddha's) reaction to extremes in wealth and physical well-being compelled him, despite a privileged up-bringing, to lead the life of an ascetic. Each of these examples reflected experiences and values that explained the centrality of emotions such as compassion, care, and love that formed the basis of opposition to injustice, exploitation, and systems or acts that treated people as means not ends.

Possibly the commentator most associated with the business-religion relationship has been Weber (1985). Hughes (1979) argued that Weber has been unfairly criticised for appearing to claim that Protestantism *caused* capitalism.

> *Weber's critics could have been spared most of their pains if they had pondered more carefully two of the author's guiding pronouncements.* (Hughes, 1979, p.329).

Weber's concerns were associated with understanding the part played by Protestantism in the spread and development of capitalism. China and Japan had some similar early capitalist signs but they had not followed the western scale of capitalist development. To support this defence of Weber, Hughes cites the following passage.

> *On the contrary, we only wish to ascertain whether and to what extent religious forces have taken part in the qualitative formation and the quantitative expansion of that spirit over the world, and what concrete aspects of our capitalist culture can be traced to them.* (Hughes, 1979, p.321).

Weber was studying a symbiotic relationship, as he saw it, not a cause and effect relationship. He referred to this symbiosis of Protestantism and capitalism as an 'elective affinity', where the largely unconscious similarities of outlook that led the second and third generations of Calvinists to put their stern ascetic capacities into the service of God's purposes on earth and, in the process, to give a new rationality and dynamism to the techniques of expanding capitalism.

Summary

Religions have been important factors in the development of business and business practices. The early experiences of religious founders appeared to shape their attitudes and beliefs about the integrity and risks associated with economic activity and it is interesting to note that usury was deemed unacceptable by both Christian and Islamic faiths (the latter arising as it did from a Christian legacy), although Christianity dropped its opposition to the practice from the mid-fifteenth century onwards. Clearly, usury was an accepted facet of trade within the Jewish faith, hence Jesus's reaction within the Temple.

The influence of religions on the business sphere has had much to do with the great wealth owned by the great religions. The Catholic Church was the dominant religion and store of wealth over centuries in Europe, with wealthy business people obtaining religious sanctions and legitimacy to their business activities by way of significant donations. However, the basic tenets of the main world religions preach values and beliefs that are invariably at odds with economic Darwinism, *homo economicus* and the primacy of worldly goods, tensions that have yet to be satisfactorily resolved.

The literature reviewed so far has considered developments, over time, of central concepts to an understanding of business in modern society. These central concepts are those of individualism, freedom, values, virtues, self-interest, justice, religion, the market, and ethical schizophrenia. Building upon this analysis, part B of this review considers contemporary issues of the 'ethics in business' debates.

ENDNOTE:

---

[1] At this time the Prophet Mohammed's uncle, Abu Talib, a tribal leader, died and Muhammad lost physical protection. The death of his wife also appeared to deepen his religious convictions.

PART B

CONTEMPORARY ISSUES IN

'*ETHICS IN BUSINESS*':

ATTEMPTS TO INFLUENCE THE POWER OF CORPORATIONS

CHAPTER SIX

CORPORATE SOCIAL RESPONSIBILITY

Corporate social responsibility (CSR), is possibly the first concept that was employed to focus public debate on both the economic and non-economic impacts of corporate activities. Different terms have also been employed to provide a focus or a greater ambit to corporations and their roles in society. Examples of alternative terminology are, corporate citizenship, business citizenship, and more latterly, corporate responsibility which is an attempt to widen the debate about the corporation's role in society.

Mitchell (1989), reported by Windsor (2001), traced the emergence of corporate social responsibility to the 1920s when concerns were growing about the scale and impact of corporate power. Mitchell (1989) casts doubt upon the motive of the development of corporate social responsibility, seeing it as a convenient device at the time to allay fears about corporate power.

Windsor (2001) suggests that more recent developments have fuelled contemporary flames. These are:

(1) The downgrading of public service delivery by public sector organisations during the Thatcher-Reagan era. During this period significant transfers of state assets and state monopolies to the private sector occurred. This privatisation and deregulation had a number of implications, including highlighting the responsibilities and accountabilities of private sector monopolies.

(2) A recognition of the evolution of a more integrated and competitive world economy. This placed a premium upon the

societal impact of organisations on their various stakeholders. Reich (1996) argued that, "electronic capitalism has replaced the gentlemanly investment system that had given 'industrial statesmen' the discretion to balance the interests of shareholders against those of employees and communities" (cited in Windsor, 2001). A 'gentlemanly investment system' is extremely questionable, viewing the past through rose-tinted spectacles. However, it can be argued that electronic communication has anaesthetised and depersonalised the process of communication.

(3)   The emphasis upon economic value and the need for all activities to be seen to be adding value, has led to the development that even corporate philanthropy had to 'add-value'. This issue was raised forcibly by Friedman (1970) and is considered below.

There have been a number of interesting developments, within the past half dozen years, that come under the banner of CSR, which include:

(1)   An ethical share index which was launched on 10 July 2001. Of the FTSE top 100 companies thirty-six corporations were not included initially in the index because they were deemed to have failed to comply with some of the index's criteria. Companies excluded included Tesco, Safeway and Royal Bank of Scotland. Some of the omissions were claimed to be due to misunderstandings, whilst companies involved in tobacco, weapons manufacture and sale, and nuclear power were not considered. Whilst the CBI expressed reservations about the index, pressure groups expressed concern at the inclusion of certain companies in the index, *eg* the Free Tibet Campaign objected to BP's inclusion. (Skorecki & Targett, 2001).

(2)   the European Union part financed an organisation named *CSR Europe*, (http://www..csreurope.org/aboutus/default.aspx) which

"launched a campaign in June 2001 (although CSR Europe came into being in 2000) to raise the sights of the Continent's business community well beyond traditional concerns for employment and labour rights" (Cowe, 2001). This last comment represented a change in intent, because the initial focus of *CSR Europe* appeared to be solely that of employment issues.

CSR Europe was intended to be the flagship of a series of campaigns that would involve a 10-nation road show, beginning in Athens in December 2001 and culminating in what was described as a 'CSR Olympics', involving awards for best practice as part of a European Year on CSR in 2005. Separate strands were aimed at boosting the teaching of 'responsible management' in business schools and enhancing the growth of socially responsible investment (SRI) funds.

Free-market critics accused CSR Europe of being anti-capitalist and anti-market. Etienne Davignon, who headed-up CSR Europe, responded, *"There is no contradiction in the term 'corporate social responsibility'. The market system is the system we have to work with. But it must be a human system and there are imperfections. We want to keep the benefits and get rid of the shortcomings"* (Cowe, 2001, p.19). Critics coming from the left of the political spectrum accused the organisation of being 'camouflage', *"allowing big business to claim responsibility without doing anything more than paying its subscriptions. Trade unionists expressed concern that the voluntarist approach could not provide sufficient protection for workers"* (Cowe, 2001, p.19).

CSR Europe came into existence with nearly fifty members, mostly multi-national corporations (MNCs) including Nike, Shell, and BP. At the time of writing this number has grown to sixty member companies, with strong relationships with national based CSR organisations, such as Business in the Community (BITC)

England and BITC Scotland; Econsense in Germany (the Forum
for Sustainable Development of Germany); Institut du Mécénat
de Solidarité in France; and Nyföcetagar Centrum (Swedish Jobs
and Society) in Sweden. Interestingly the Personnel Director of
BT, a member of *CSR Europe,* offered the following definition
of corporate social responsibility. "It is about doing business in a
way that persuades our customers to buy from us, our employees
to work hard for us and our communities to accept us" (Cowe,
2001, p.19).

Although Carr (1968), raised concerns about the underlying
ethicality of business leaders, Baumol (1958), Berle (1958), Besser
(2002), Friedman and Friedman (1962 and 1980) provided a more
reasoned defence of the need for businesses to be exempt from the
burdens of non-economic responsibilities. However, Friedman's most
cited publication on this subject was the article he wrote for the *New
York Times Magazine* in 1970. The article was a response to what were
becoming increasingly frequent calls for corporations to act in socially
responsible ways in the late 1960s and early 1970s. Precisely what was
meant by 'socially responsible' was often left vague and poorly explained,
save for concerns being expressed that corporate power was authority
without responsibility, and that corporations were able to avoid a
number of costs of their operations, because costs such as pollution
clean-ups, and environmental and social damage costs were not charged
to the organisations concerned, but paid for by various communities
and societies. Business corporations were effectively being subsidised.
Where the law allowed penalty costs to be awarded, the decision as to
whether to introduce improved pollution controls within a company,
for example, seemed too often to be an economic calculation (*ie* cost
of pollution controls *versus* penalty costs if successfully prosecuted),
rather than an ethically-based decision. There have been individual
case examples that have been used to debate and illuminate complex
business-society issues, such as those reported in Donaldson and

Werhane (1979); Goodpaster (1983); Hoffman and Moore (1984); Luthans *et al.*, 1987; Matthews *et al.* (1991); and Sawyer (1979), but corporate social responsibility remains a contested and problematic concept (Reich, 1998).

Friedman's criticisms were rehearsed by Wolf (2000) thirty years after the publication of Friedman's article. Wolf accused those (still) calling for greater corporate social responsibility as not only distorting business activity, but confusing and misunderstanding the rationale of business. "The role of well run companies is to make profits, not save the planet", Wolf argued.

Friedman criticised those who urged corporations to act in ways that could be described as socially responsible, on three fronts. The first criticism was an economic one, with ethical undertones. If corporations were required to engage in corporate philanthropy, such as making donations to charities, schools or hospitals, such acts would distort allocative efficiency, or the efficiency with which capital was employed. If this was to happen then the principal indicator of corporate performance would be distorted and investment decisions would be denied a rational basis. Friedman argued that corporations were responsible for using shareholders' funds in profitable ways. Worrying about which charity to support, or which good deed(s) to perform, merely 'takes management's eye off the ball'; the ball being how to increase profits.

Baumol (1975) supported Friedman's view, criticising those who sought to impose 'non-economic ethics' upon corporations. For Baumol, "the merciless market is the consumer's best friend" (Phelps, 1975, p.46). Voluntary supererogation would only hurt the well-intentioned but misguided business. Thus, the only form of corporate philanthropy that Friedman's argument would accept was where it could be shown that a donation, or good deed, would improve a company's profitability in superior ways to other ways of spending that same sum of money. This approach has been described as 'prudential altruism': a calculating and instrumental act that would not be repeated if the underlying self-interest was not satisfied within the prescribed time period (Windsor, 2001). However, this was a very 'particular' form of altruism. In such a case the charitable donation would be more accurately described as a commercial investment. Prudent altruism was at one level a cynical use of language, but on the other it revealed the level of ethicality at which the debate would be operating if prudent altruism was indeed the motive behind a corporate donation.

An alternative phrase to prudent altruism was that of 'corporate philanthropy' as used by Porter and Kramer (2002). Porter took issue with organisations that indulged in unthoughtful or wasteful altruism (not Porter's phrases). Examples included organisations that made donations to charities or good causes with no obvious link between the organisation and the charity or good cause. Such acts were examples of altruistic behaviour, or a gift made with no instrumental intent. Porter and Kramer's (2002) notion of strategic philanthropy was that, with more thought, they could contribute to the well-being of communities and societies by helping themselves. An example would be for a travel company to sponsor the development of tourism-related programmes of study in colleges and universities, particularly in areas where education provision might be below the national average.

Whether such examples are genuinely altruistic may be seen as merely a semantic point, but possibly it is not. Maybe Porter and Kramer's examples reflect a more reasoned approach to what corporations can be reasonably expected to do under the banner of corporate (social) responsibility. Whether the investment by the travel organisation will represent an appropriate type of educational programme for young people is not considered within this debate. The approach seems to be, "some education is better than no education", but the uncritical acceptance of such acts as philanthropy is a use of the term that does not seem compatible with its traditional usage, but such is how the meaning of words mutates into 'new' meanings.

The law in America and the UK requires limited liability business entities to operate on behalf of shareholders and although advisory statements emanating from government departments and influential regulatory and professional bodies sometimes encourage corporations to act in broad societal interests, these judgements are all discretionary. This issue is picked up in the second of Friedman's defences.

The second of Friedman's criticisms drew upon both ethics and political philosophy where it was undemocratic for corporations to use shareholders funds to support charities or other 'good causes'. Any such donation could only come at the expense of lower dividends, higher prices, or lower wages, or a combination of all three. Friedman asked how it could be ethical that a corporation should act first as unpaid tax collector, levying a tax on the shareholders, customers and/or employees, and then as unaccountable benefactor? Publicly elected representatives of the people (national or local politicians) should provide financial support to public services or charities, from public funds, or individuals should decide to which charities they personally wished to make private donations. A further objection to such donations, which Friedman did not make, was that social institutions, such as schools and hospitals that relied on corporate donations placed the education and health of citizens at the whim of market variability and volatility. These were unsound financial foundations for the provision of such critical services (see Seedhouse, 1988).

The third criticism was a philosophical one; corporations could not possess such responsibilities because corporations were social constructs, brought into existence by societies passing laws that gave legal protection to certain forms of business associations and structures. Without these legal and social devices, corporations could not, and would not, exist. In Friedman's terms only individuals could have responsibilities, not corporations. Windsor (2001) notes:

> *The corporate citizenship notion conflates citizen (which a firm cannot be) and person (which a firm can be, but only as a legal*

fiction). The portrayal is fictional in that, although for many purposes a corporation is treated in law as if a person with rights of private contracting, public expression and political activities, the corporation cannot vote or hold office, not even through agents – the key hallmarks of citizenship defined as a share in sovereign power in a democratic polity. … . Fictional personhood is not a sound basis for artificial citizenship. (p.41).

Windsor's reference to firms being treated in law as 'persons' was reflected in two legal cases reported by Shaw and Barry (1998). The first case was First National Bank of Boston *v* Bellotti and the second a 1996 case in which the US Supreme Court unanimously overturned a Rhode Island law which had stood for 40 years. In both cases the American courts supported corporations using the American Constitution's protection of freedom of speech to allow the corporations to make particular statements, notwithstanding that the American Constitution was constructed to protect the rights of individual American citizens, not corporations. The courts, themselves a social construct, were thereby granting corporations the rights of citizens, at least in the context of freedom of speech. Thus, Friedman's third objection has been overridden by the American courts and business itself. But the treatment of corporations as citizens may not be a satisfactory development and may have unforeseeable unintended consequences.

Crane and Matten (2004) considered a range of reasons why corporations should have responsibilities beyond, and in addition to, their shareholders including:

(1) corporations can cause social problems and must therefore accept responsibility for these actions;

(2) corporations have a moral responsibility to use the resources at their disposal and the considerable power they wield in responsible ways; and

(3) corporations are invariably part of formal or informal networks (stakeholder groups) and a responsibility lies with all stakeholders to be aware of, and respect, the ramifications of their actions on others.

Crane and Matten also cite Carroll (1979, 1991) and Carroll and Buchholtz (2000), by referring to Carroll's four part framework of CSR. This was an attempt by Carroll to think more critically about corporate responsibility and to analyse the concept into different types of responsibility.

- The first two stages of corporate responsibility, economic responsibility and legal responsibility, were *required by society*. The corporation had to exhibit behaviour that conformed to the economic imperative placed upon directors of corporations to act, primarily, in the interests of shareholders that was enshrined in (UK) company law.

- Ethical responsibility was *expected by society*. However, developments in employment conditions and human rights (*eg* the European Court of Human Rights) were converting what were once discretionary behaviours on the part of corporations into legal obligations and demonstrated the dynamism of CSR. The market-based, capital-dependent economy is a dynamic concept, and, as Micklethwait and Wooldridge (2003) observe, shows a remarkable resilience in changing and evolving to respond to differing social pressures.

- Philanthropic responsibility was *desired by society*. The prospect of philanthropic responsibility being desired by society is contentious, and not just from a Friedmanite position. If an organisation such as a school, hospital or hospice, became dependent upon a corporate donor or donors, a potentially vital element of civil society would be at risk of a general or specific economic downturn in the markets. Public services should have public, not private, funding to ensure the continuity of basic civil and human rights. These are moral arguments, not indisputable facts, but they reflect the level of mature, complex and problematic debates that societies need to engage with if the outcomes are not to be determined by powerful elites, corporate or otherwise.

Attempts to improve ex-post accountability

Initiatives under the banner of social responsibility accounting came principally from academics in the 1960s and 1970s, but in 1975 the UK Accounting Standards Steering Committee published *The Corporate Report*, which was the response of the professional accountancy bodies to the growing clamour (amongst academics at least) for reporting corporate activities beyond those that were of concern to shareholders. The environmental accounting movement is of more recent vintage (*eg* Gray, 1992), with information on the impact of organisational activity on the environment. Both of these developments are largely associated with ex-post reporting. They are not concerned with integrating stakeholder perspectives into decision-making processes, although by increasing the amount of disclosure required of companies in terms of their social and environmental impact, supporters of these initiatives argue that scrutiny will be enhanced and the debate better informed. Indeed one of the UK professional accountancy bodies, ACCA, makes an annual award for the 'best' environmental report by a company.

Holland and Gibbon (2001) provide an overview of various frameworks for environmental reporting, including those produced by:

• the Chartered Association of Certified Accountants (ACCA), *'Making Values Count'* (Gonella et al., 1998);

- the *Institute for Social and Ethical Accountability* in 1999 (AccountAbility Standard 1000);

- a discussion paper on a proposed framework for environmental reporting, from the *Fédération des Experts Comptables Européens* (FEE), in 1999;

- the Global Reporting Initiative (GRI), of the Coalition for Environmentally Responsible Economies (CERES), also in 1999; and

- a set of guidance rules issued by the International Organisation for Standardisation (ISO) known as ISO 14000.

A recent approach to enhancing the scope and perspective of the corporate reports has been the development of a 'triple bottom line' approach (Belal, 2002; Elkington, 1999; and Elkington and Fennell, 2000), which encompasses economic, social and environmental concerns, rather than the traditional focus upon economic performance and accounting profits. However, operationalisation of the triple bottom line remains problematic. Explanations of what is meant by 'triple bottom line' suggest that an equal weighting is not being given to the three elements. Birch (2001), in reviewing a draft charter of corporate citizenship developed by *BP Australia*, refers to a statement contained within the draft charter under the heading 'sustainable development'.

BP is committed to a socially, environmentally and economically responsible business. This means maximising profit in order to create wealth and sustainable jobs, always intending to have a positive social and environmental impact. (Birch, 2001, p.62).

The reference to maximising profit is interesting. Within the draft charter no attempt is made to discuss the tension between this commitment and the commitment made to the social and the environmental issues mentioned elsewhere in the draft charter.

However, Birch refers to earlier discussions with *BP Australia* during which these issues appear to have been raised:

> *The tensions between capitalism and democracy as currently defined are irreconcilable without serious change. We agreed that we could not achieve long-term sustainability without change. Business needs, therefore, significant policy directions to enable this change to occur, not just within business practices but also within society overall.* (Birch, 2001, p.59).

The phrase, 'business needs … significant policy directions' refers directly to the need for a policy directive by governments, because businesses cannot be expected to act unilaterally if such actions are likely to lead to competitive disadvantage or worse. The 'hidden-hand' of the market is viewed as too unreliable to be left to its own devices in this context.

Summary

CSR is a concept that has a longevity of some eighty years. Since the mid-1990s a number of other terms have been tabled to try and either sharpen its focus or to broaden it, but in both respects such attention suggests that CSR has been pulled in so many directions that it has lost something in its various translations. There has been a long-standing and fundamental disagreement concerning the wisdom, sense and morality of economic entities being required to perform non-economic functions. To this day the arguments continue.

CHAPTER SEVEN

THE STAKEHOLDER AND SUSTAINABILITY

Stakeholding

Stakeholding, can be compartmentalised into one of two camps. The first relates stakeholding as the basis of enlightened self-interest. The arguments are that it pays to adopt a stakeholder approach where gains can be made because, if not, competitors will (Jones, 1995). The second group advocates a stakeholding perspective on non-consequentialist grounds (Clarkson, 1994, 1995; Evan & Freeman, 1988, 1993; and Freeman, 1984). Mitchell *et al.* (1997) provide an overview of the various arguments.

One of the early signs in the UK of corporations moving beyond an exclusive shareholder focus (although the reality of the latter was formerly challenged, amongst others, by Berle and Means in 1932), was the Christian Frontier Council (CFC). The CFC was established in 1939, although it did not meet formally until 1942. The Council was, at that time, made up of senior figures from the worlds of politics, the Christian Church and business and the rationale for its advocacy of a stakeholding perspective for organisations reflected a principled, non-consequentialist stance. The foundation of the association was to discuss the application of Christian beliefs and direct society towards Christian influences and to cooperate with groups attempting to promote similar ideas (Marinetto, 1999).

Marinetto (1999) argued that the Council could lay claim, to "having influenced George Goyder's seminal texts, *The Future of Private*

Enterprise and *The Responsible Company"* (Marinetto, 1999). In the first 1951 text Goyder advocated the use of cooperative structures within organisations, with directors holding the position of trustees, whilst in the second text *The Responsible Company* (1961), he advocated changes in the law to require companies to introduce democratic governance structures. Both texts spoke of stakeholders as shareholders, employees, consumers, the local community and society at large. The movement beyond shareholders and employees as being the key stakeholders reflected both the predominate arguments coming from the CFC, and also the greater social awareness of the business–society relationship, fuelled by the egalitarian seeds that the Second World War had sown. Goyder's ideas represented a shift away from neo-classical assumptions of organisational focus, supported by a group of senior Christian businessmen, but stayed within a market-based, capitalist-dependent, economic structure.

The Future of Private Enterprise was published soon after the end of the Second World War, but the orientation and arguments of the publication cannot be ascribed merely to the political and social climate of the time. The CFC was established by J H Oldham, who Marinetto described as:

> *A missionary and ecumenical leader, who moved in the same circles as* [Archbishop] *Temple in the 1930s. Both were involved in the Life and Work conferences which sought to bring Christian ethics to social and economic structures of society, particularly businesses.* (Marinetto, 1999, p.2).

The Life and Work conferences were a reflection of the concerns of the times, particularly following the great depression years of the late 1920s and 1930s. Yet, concerns about the business–society relationship were not confined to periods of economic depression. The 1950s and 1960s were, relatively speaking, more prosperous and optimistic years, yet Thurrow (1982) was still moved to say:

Paradoxically, at precisely the time when capitalism finds itself with no social competitors – its former competitors, socialism and communism having died – it will have to undergo a profound metamorphosis. (p.15).

These are prophetic words, given that they were written nearly forty years ago. The so-called iron curtain was not finally torn down until the very late 1980s and the official demise of communism could not be announced until that time. Yet Thurrow felt able to declare the triumph of capitalism over socialism and communism before then, but more importantly he recognised, even in capitalism's 'victory', the critical need for it to transform, or be transformed, and not just in small incremental steps.

The use of the term 'social competitors', not just economic competitors, recognises the description of capitalism as a social system, and not just an economic system. If capitalism was accepted as a social system and not just an economic system that challenged the values of prevailing social systems, then the claims for greater inclusivity in corporate decision making began to possess greater robustness against neo-liberal critics.

The 1970s was a period when the talk was of 'industrial democracy', when the National Enterprise Board was set-up, and even the Conservative Government of Edward Heath published a White Paper on *Company Law Reform*, in which proposals were made for the creation of a code of conduct to stimulate a wider sense of responsibility in the business community. At the same time articles were published with greater frequency on the theme of the social responsibilities of business, *eg* Beesley, (1974); Beesley and Evans, (1978); BIM, (1974); CBI, (1973); Ivens, (1970); Kempner *et al.,* (1974); Robertson, (1974); Fogarty, (1975); Epstein, (1976 and 1977); Humble, (1976); SSRC, (1976); and Shenfield, (1971).

Drawing upon the work of Van Luijk (1990), Vogel (1992: 1998) and Enderle (1996), Crane and Matten (2004) identified six differences between the American and continental European approaches towards business ethics. The major distinction was that the role of the individual reflected a multiple stakeholder approach in Europe, whilst the American approach 'focused upon shareholder value'. This acceptance of multiple stakeholders was most obviously evident in Germany, The Netherlands and Denmark, with their adoption of two tier boards where the supervisory boards represented the interests of employees and external (non-equity) financiers. However, the increasing dominance of American financial markets and the corporate governance orientation adopted by the OECD that mirrored the Anglo/American approach, indicates a trend towards market-based forms of corporate governance rather than relational-based approaches used in continental Europe and Japan (Rose and Mejer, 2003).

The UK approach is much closer to the American model in terms of board structure and its composition, notably the use and roles of non-executive directors. Responsibility for ethical conduct in business in America relies upon the 'individual', compared to the European approach where 'social control by the collective' is argued to be the orientation (Crane and Matten, 2004). The UK perspective does not place exclusive responsibility upon the individual, although the latter is still important. There is greater acceptance amongst writers on UK affairs that structural issues are important factors affecting ethics in business (eg Amoore, 2002; Andriof, 2001; Hutton, 2002; and McIntosh, et al., 2003; Slapper and Tombs, 1999).

The Christian Frontier Council, whilst built upon Christian principles, was a movement firmly rooted in practice. A slightly more idealistic approach was reflected in the 1924 Hibbert lectures presented by L P Jacks. These lectures possessed a broader sweep than corporate social responsibility or stakeholding, but in the lectures Jacks laid down a series of challenges, to individuals, to society at large, and to labour in the form of [pride in] workmanship. The underlying beliefs that informed Jacks' position were those of the interdependency and symbiosis between human beings. If these lectures were to be repeated today a set of challenges would no doubt be tabled for 'business'. Describing such challenges as idealistic can be interpreted by some as idealistic challenges not rooted in the real world. This is not the intention. Idealistic arguments can provide essential benchmarks against which actual performance can be compared. Many would argue that the challenges facing modern societies in terms of sustainability, social cohesion and political stability scream out with their rootedness in the 'real world'. The imperatives that confront modern societies are not merely moral, but it can be argued that they address the very continuity and sustainability of the human race.

Sustainability

Initially sustainability was explored via the economic perspective (Arrow and Hurwicz, 1977; Meadows *et al.* 1974; Daly, 1991; Daly and Cobb, 1989; Pearce, 1999), with social sustainability tending to lag economic analyses, although Hirsch (1977) was a notable exception.

Employing a stakeholder perspective, sustainability is normally defined as the application of resources for contemporary benefit that does not prejudice or compromise the interests of future generations. This treats natural resources as resources at the disposal of societies, but with social choices invariably (and particularly within modern fractured societies) heavily influenced, if not dictated by, influential corporate interests.

Advocates of the neo-liberalist perspective are exemplified in the writings of Rand (Hull and Peikoff, 1999); Friedman (1970); and Friedman and Friedman (1962; 1980), who take an ethical egoist stance to make three fundamental assumptions. The first concerns markets that are assumed to be close to, or approaching, perfect market conditions, where any disequilibrium conditions are assumed to be temporary and correctable. The second concerns voice, where all individuals possess access to democratic institutions and structures to enable them to express their concerns and have their views understood and considered. The third concerns choice about freedom over where individuals live and the behaviour they adopt. The most critical of these elements, from a neo-liberalist position, is that of markets because, if many of the activities in which people participate are coordinated *via* the operation of competitive markets, including heath care, education, housing, and the law, the resulting levels of service, quality, and distribution will reflect societal preferences.

This crucial assumption concerning the efficiency and effectiveness of markets has been questioned by various writers, but most recently by Stiglitz (2000, 2002, 2003). Stiglitz questions the ability of many markets to function at tolerable levels of equity because of information asymmetries, and even if this was possible, from a sustainability perspective the considerations and deliberations of free-marketers on current decisions for future generations is missing. The ethical underpinning of perfectly competitive markets is that they are amoral, but the wishes and choices of future generations are mute at the tables of corporate decision makers. If the outcomes arising from the forces of supply and demand are assumed to represent the moral (as well as economic) choices of society via the 'hidden hand', the interests of future generations can only be brought into business decisions if ethics and values are introduced, particularly justice.

An interesting movement which was founded in 1989 by the Swedish oncologist, Karl-Henrik Robèrt is '*The Natural Step*'. Robèrt had become concerned at significant increases in childhood leukaemia and traced the causes to increasing toxins in the environment due to human production processes (see also Satchel, 1994). Robèrt's investigations resulted in him being concerned that environmental debates concentrated too heavily upon the effects of methods of producing goods, rather than looking at more fundamental issues, such as the systemic causes of environmental problems. To challenge the debates of the time Robèrt established *The Natural Step* organisation in Sweden. Wider interest followed across Europe and in 1995 the organisation established a base in America.

The Natural Step is an organisation committed to sustainable communities. Its ethos is embodied in four core principles:

1. Reducing the use of critical mineral resources: by mineral substitution; by the development of synthetic substitutes; and/or by being far more efficient in the extraction process and the use of scarce minerals.

2. Eliminating concentrations of problematic substances such as the substitution of compounds with long half-lives that represent a threat to life. Substitutes should be non-(or less) toxic and be far more bio-degradable.

3. Minimising natural resource utilisation such as using resources that are renewable (*eg* forests). Well-managed eco-systems should be a part of life. Where resources are not renewable then far greater caution has to be exercised, and may cause property rights to become a crucial issue.

4. Using resources efficiently, fairly and responsibly so that the needs of all people, and the future needs of people who are not yet born, stand the best chance of being met. (www.thenaturalstep.org)

Nature – a reconsideration of stakeholding

The stakeholder debates tend to place environmental issues outside the stakeholder group. This 'type' of stakeholding can be referred to as the stakeholder-within perspective. The stakeholder-within perspective is located at the organisational level where all the stakeholders have a (vested) interest in the continuity of the corporation, in one form or another. However, 'nature' is treated as a resource, at the disposal of the corporation, subject to social norms and laws. If, for example, an opportunity exists for an organisation to legally drill for mineral deposits in an area of outstanding natural beauty, and not do so would involve redundancies, the organisation that adopts a stakeholding-within approach, involving the views of the employees and other 'immediate' stakeholders, will chose to drill.

A different perspective would be taken by the stakeholder-outwith (objective stakeholding) perspective. This refers to the stakeholder who is indifferent about the continuity of the organisation, not antagonistic, just indifferent. The organisation touches them only in so far as the corporation impacts upon the natural environment. The individuals have no vested interest in the decision beyond this relationship. *The Natural Step* movement reflects this position.

The objective-stakeholder perspective places the stakeholder outside the corporation, and does not consider the corporation as the principal point of focus. This is a fundamental change from the normal orientation of the stakeholder perspective. The general schema represented by the objective-stakeholder is essentially a pluralist one, with the corporation as only one of many interested parties.

The objective-stakeholder perspective challenges the often taken-for-granted assumption that individuals are distinct from, and independent of, nature. Whilst the Friedmanite position is that corporations should not be expected to behave in socially responsible ways, beyond legal compliance, a phenomenological perspective would argue that corporations *cannot* be expected to behave in socially responsible ways, beyond complying with the law of the land. This is because a corporation cannot employ a value system beyond instrumentality, certainly not while company law identifies shareholder interests as the exclusive concern of managers. Thus, if new relationships are to be defined between corporations and the citizenry, these will need to be addressed at many levels.

The Cartesian division of the world into subjects and objects was challenged by Husserl (1965), and developed by Heidegger (1978) and

Merleau-Ponty (Silverman, 1988 and Silverman *et al.* 1988). Rather than just bracketing scientific explanations of the world as Husserl suggested, Heidegger rejected scientific claims as being objective and unproblematic. He saw the supposed quest for scientific understanding as a mask for man's desire to control and dominate nature, using it in an exclusively exploitative relationship. Exploitation is an accusation that can be laid at the feet of corporations and governments in both capitalist and non-capitalist systems, when the sole (official) *raison d'être* of an organisation is that of making money, where financial markets around the world place considerable strains upon long-term economic decision making, and the only value system that could be brought to corporate decision making is that of instrumentality. In such a context nature is seen, purely and simply, as a resource, or a standing reserve as Heidegger would classify it.

One of Heidegger's great concerns was with "revealing", what he referred to as an object's essence. How an object was revealed was dependent upon the perceiver. Thus, there was more than one way of perceiving an object, and more than one way in which the object could be revealed. An example illustrates 'revealing', and the fundamental distinction between the stakeholder-within and objective-stakeholder perspectives.

A site of special interest, whether that interest be scientific, cultural, social or environmental, may possess certain attributes that are of particular interest to business corporations. The attributes might be diamonds, timber, uranium, oil, the potential for property development or tourism. To local people the site might represent special cultural and spiritual relevance, or a symbol or a source of continuity with the past and with the future. The site might also represent a symbol of bygone atrocities, or be a scene of great heroism, possessing a symbolic relevance that transcends the local community and interests the public. If one is in touch with these histories, the site might reflect not so much a grouping of trees, hills, parkland, or whatever the physical attributes of the site, but rather the site might be revealed as representing qualities of human activity that need protecting and cherishing[1]. Certain locations hold memories, symbolise human achievements or reveal lessons for the future and are the direct result of earlier civilisations' uses of nature. But nature is in a dynamic state of evolution and renewal, albeit when measured in geological time. The essence of the phenomenological debate is not the untouchability of nature, but thinking that leads to the decision, to use, to deploy or to exploit nature. It is in this context that Heidegger's 'enframing of technology' is key.

Heidegger was not anti-technology, indeed, it was not technology that was the focus of his disdain for the limitations of instrumentality. His concern was with the enframing of technology, the technological mindset, the technological mentality, wherein nature could only ever be perceived as what it could yield, what it could become, what it could be converted to as a means to an end. The end would commonly be money, but it could also be non-pecuniary power.

From a Heideggerian perspective, the value of an object is not the object itself, but the relationship that exists between a subject and an object. The existence of a relationship means that there is a history to explain that relationship and a memory to draw upon and articulate that history. However, there is an important caveat. The above discussion suggests a relationship between a specific subject and a specific object. For the argument to have more environmental relevance there needs to be a relationship between a subject and a broader concept that the object represents, such as the spirituality of a place, or wilderness, rather than just the single object. Thus, the history might come from particular experiences such as travel, stories, ancestors, an empathy with nature born from experiences in the formative years, that are then generalisable to broader issues. This reflects an intrinsic value and a non-instrumental value. To possess intrinsic value, an object must possess either some form of economic value beyond its functional value, and/or it requires a past. The major problem with this value is that it might limit an object's intrinsic value to some form of 'objective' physical, economic factor. However, an intrinsic value that is limited to a generalisable, economic expression is unduly restrictive. Non-instrumental, non-economic value has also to be understood[2].

The need for a history between a subject and an object raises fundamental problems for corporations and the stakeholder-within perspective. Where, or with whom, does the corporate memory reside? How are values determined, inculcated, reviewed, re-assessed and communicated? By whom? To whom? How does a corporation, or a stakeholder-within perspective determine a non-economic, intrinsic value?

The nature of "Being" for a corporation is essentially an economic one. In a resource constrained world where the laws of property rights and capitalist modes of production form the bedrock of corporate activity, it cannot be otherwise. Bringing multiple perspectives into corporate decision making might be an improvement upon the myopic shareholder focus, but it still represents a very partial *and biased* stakeholder perspective with two problematic issues – the nature of "Being" and the status of the corporation.

Individuals are not essentially or irrevocably economic actors. The actual nature of a "Being" is a contestable one. Whether the *raison d'être* of corporations is an exclusive shareholder orientation, or a more inclusive focus, the economic objective has to remain a primary concern. Where instrumentality is the determinant of value. There is no relationship between subject (the corporation) and object, other than that of instrumentality. Indeed when the corporation is placed as the subject, rather than the individual, then individual members of society cease to be subjects and become objects. Thus, individuals become means to ends *via* the objectification of subjects, which Marx referred to as the commodification of man. The nature of corporate "Being" is thus a singular one, with no justification beyond the economic.

The second internal tension of the stakeholder-within perspective relates to the placing of the corporation at the centre of the debate over the use of nature and human rights. Stakeholder groups are usually identified as shareholders; employees; customers; suppliers; local constituencies; government and civil society; and future societies. The ordering of these groups is intentional, in that the views and interests of the latter mentioned groups are less easily obtained. Thus, a stakeholder-within perspective is likely to preference the interests of the shareholders, employees; customers; and suppliers, with the interests of local constituencies also coming into play from time to time. Whilst these interests are not always at one with one another, they are invariably co-terminus in seeing the continuance of the specific corporation as important. Whilst the 'markets' might be indifferent as to which corporations prosper and which expire, the type of stakeholders mentioned above are extremely unlikely to be indifferent. They will want to protect their respective vested interests. Thus, the ethics of exploiting locations of cheap overseas labour, or the destruction of areas of great environmental or geological importance, or the trading with governments with troublesome human rights records, might be seen in a different light when the implications of ethical or holistic decision making threatens local jobs.

The stakeholder-within perspective is skewed towards those vested interests with immediate access to the decision-making table. The stakeholder-within perspective holds onto a Cartesian view of the world and in other than exceptional cases nature will remain a resource to be used, being revealed only through instrumental notions of value. On its own the stakeholder-within perspective cannot provide a sufficiently robust theory of a societally-inclusive stakeholder perspective.

Even the tools of analysis and the philosophical basis of decision-making within the stakeholder-within perspective are contentious. Weiss (1998) comments:

Corporations are socially and morally responsible to their constituencies to the extent they maintain responsible relationships with their stakeholders and respond to their legitimate rights and claims according to ethical standards of fairness and justice, **as well as to utilitarian costs and benefits analyses** [emphasis added] (p.99).

Cost benefit analysis (CBA) reflects a belief that all salient elements to a debate can be satisfactorily reduced to a quantitative expression. Yet numbers are notoriously inarticulate. Even the philosophical base of CBA is a distorted version of utilitarianism. When Mill (Williams, 1976) discussed utilitarianism and its principal criterion, the maximisation of happiness (which was then interpreted as pleasure, although Mill was not comfortable with Bentham's use of the term utility), he expressly differentiated between different forms of pleasure. Mill argued, in keeping with the ancient Greek philosophers, that gaining pleasure or happiness through intellectual pursuits were of a higher order than physical pleasures, and although he accepted that in any dispute between the ranking of two pleasures, the one that gives the greatest pleasure to the greatest number has to have the higher rank, he made an important caveat. The people expressing their preferences could do so only as, "… competently acquainted with both [choices]". They need to be, "equally acquainted with, and equally capable of appreciating and enjoying both [choices]". This is important because Mill did not consider all expressions of pleasure by a variety of people to be of equal weight. Permanent pleasure (happiness) is of less value if the pleasures being enjoyed are considered to be of low value. Thus, some displeasure is acceptable, because it can be a necessary condition of appreciating the higher pleasures. "It is better to be a human being dissatisfied than a pig satisfied; better to be Socrates dissatisfied than a fool satisfied. And if the fool or the pig are of a different opinion, it is only because they only know their own side of the question". (Williams, 1976).

Corporations have to take decisions, from time to time, that can negatively affect the most obvious and vocal stakeholders. In philosophical terms this has to be the case, but can actual practice be relied upon to deliver foresightedness, wisdom and altruism[3]? The issue of vested interests in keeping an organisation going are an intriguing part of the stakeholder debate. What are the criteria for deciding that an organisation is, or is not, socially useful? The stakeholder-within perspective can only offer a very biased view.

However, the objective-stakeholder perspective does not fully overcome these limitations. Heidegger argued that significant power imbalances exist within society; that information asymmetry exists on a significant scale; that a technology mentality persists; and that individuals fail to respect their responsibilities of being citizens. But these limitations also apply to the stakeholder-within position. The objective-stakeholder perspective offers more potential than the stakeholder-within perspective as it does not accept a technology mentality, but neither does it reject technology. The focus of the objective-stakeholder is that of societies within nature with a phenomenological view of the world, rather than a Cartesian one. Corporations are important within the evolutionary development of societies, but they do not dominate thinking or action. This may seem idealistic, maybe unrealistic, but some manifestations of such a perspective are evident in contemporary life. An objective-stakeholder perspective manifests itself in far greater consumer reaction to corporate practices; protests (not just consumers) against corporate mis-behaviour; a greater challenging of government action over the support given to corporate business; stronger laws to protect natural resources and human rights worldwide; and different orientations to the teaching of business decision-making in universities[4]. Examples exist of all of these actions/reactions in recent years.

Summary

The concept of stakeholding has enjoyed attention over many decades, but this chapter has pointed to an important limitation of the traditional view of stakeholding. This refers to the fact that the 'normal' stakeholding groups, such as shareholders; employees; customers; suppliers; and local communities have vested interests in the continuation of the firm. This is referred to as the 'stakeholder-within' perspective.

An alternative perspective is the 'stakeholder-outwith' perspective. This refers to a perspective analogous to Adam Smith's 'stranger' or 'spectator', in that the stakeholder-outwith' perspective represents an objective, disinterested view on what the objectively correct decision should be in any given situation particularly involving the environment. In the latter context the interests of general society and future societies are invariably inadequately represented in the stakeholder-within perspective, if they are represented at all.

One possible way forward in achieving an inclusive perspective on the part of decision makers is possibly to gain acceptance of the organisation, and those who are charged with decision making powers, as if they were citizens of the states in which they operate and affect. This is the focus of the next chapter.

ENDNOTES:

---

[1] Cherishing is an interesting concept. The more people cherish things the less they will want to replace them. However, markets depend on people wanting to replace things. There have even been attempts to market cherishing, to make money out of people's desire to cherish, to possess cherished objects (*eg* mementos and souvenirs).

[2] The florin is a case in point. The florin possessed a face value equivalent to 10p, but at various times it actually contained traces of silver. Thus, there were times, depending upon the price of silver, when the coin's intrinsic economic value

could exceed its face value. However, in centuries, or millennia to come, the non-economic, intrinsic value could be significant in archaeological terms.

3   Altruism which provides an overall (societal) benefit fits within a utilitarian perspective (recognising the utilitarian distinction between the morality of action and the morality of motive), but whether it would be allowed to exist politically in the stakeholder-within corporation is extremely debatable.

4   If such possibilities can emerge, then fundamental changes will need to go beyond actual practice. The assumptions that underpin economics, accounting and financial management techniques within corporate decision making will require changes in business schools at both undergraduate and postgraduate levels. But even then, any attempt to embrace broader stakeholder perspectives is unlikely to be able to address the issues raised by Heidegger. To do so would require an understanding of nature, a perspective on nature, a relationship with nature, which is diametrically opposed to that which is implicit within current models of decision making. At present the most that can be anticipated on business and management programmes at undergraduate and postgraduate levels are modules on environmental issues taught separately from time-honoured approaches to business decision making taught within the core programme modules. The core modules reflect the dominant (often the exclusive) business paradigm presented to prospective and current managers.

Chapter Eight

The Corporation as Citizen

During the mid-1990s the concepts of corporate social responsibility and stakeholder-type perspectives became too limited and thus, the more inclusive, holistic concept of citizenship was conceived. Crane and Matten (2004) suggest that business practitioners saw CSR and Business Ethics as too patronising or critical. The development of the argument from one of requiring corporations to act in socially responsible ways, to calls for corporations to be 'citizens', can be seen as a desire to back corporations, both conceptually and legally, into the responsibilities that this status would confer. However, the work of writers such as Arora (2002); Carroll (1998); Maignan, (2001); Maignan and Ferrell (2000, 2001); Maignan et al. (1999); Waddell (2000); and Zadek et al. (1997) took corporate citizenship a little further than the arguments that had been used to explain, justify and operationalise corporate social responsibility, because citizenship confers rights as well as responsibilities upon corporations.

Wood and Logsdon (2001) consider this question and argue that corporations can be assigned responsibilities, but rights are a different matter. From this perspective corporations are seen as important and powerful players within the development of societies, but they are not 'real' persons, linking back to Friedman's (1970) arguments against corporations being required to assume social responsibilities. However, the Wood and Logsdon-type argument is quite distinct from that of Friedman. In the former case corporations have responsibilities but limited rights and have a 'license to operate', based upon a social contract, which is discussed in chapter eleven.

The term citizen normally relates to the relationship between individuals and the political state in which they live. It carries with it notions of rights and responsibilities on the part of individuals and the state. However, this reciprocity is unlikely to be an equal one. Within democratic theories of the state, citizens have ultimate sovereignty over the state, or at least sovereignty over those who represent the citizenry within government. To bring corporations within the idea of 'the citizenry' poses fundamental challenges.

Being described as a citizen does not of itself infer much about morality. It is a noun in need of an adjective such as 'good' or 'moral' before it can confer a positive societal influence. Wood and Logsdon (2001) referred to this issue when they observed that:

> One important debate distinguishes the concept of citizenship-as-legal-status from the concept of citizen-as-desirable-activity. The minimum requirements to be called a citizen are very different from the requirement to be called a 'good citizen'. (p.88).

The role of the citizen can vary from the active notion of citizenship evident in ancient Greece (for those conferred as free men), to a passive acceptance of governance from a sovereign body (à la Hobbes) or from the bureaucratic state (à la Weber). Within the corporate citizen debate, the demands made of corporations vary from a minimalist societally-neutral influence, to a pro-active role. The societally-neutral arguments do not, however, reflect a *status-quo* situation, or even a single understanding of what might be meant by societally-neutral. For example, would being societally–neutral mean that:

• negative and positive effects of corporate activities could be balanced out (possibly involving an international perspective), and that a corporation's impact would not harm anyone or anything?;

- acting within legal constraints is acceptable, even if the law is judged by many to be inadequate (as a result of the political lobbying by corporations); and

- a general acceptance that corporations have social responsibilities.

In modern democratic societies, although the citizenry possesses theoretical sovereignty over the state, in practice the citizenry has little or no access to certain sources of information and knowledge. Without an effective and rigorous freedom of information act (Vickers, 2002), the citizenry is at a disadvantage to its elected representatives, and they in turn at a disadvantage to the Executive. In terms of corporations, the only relationship between individuals and corporations that is recognised at law is that of shareholder, consumer, employee or commercial operator, but no relationship is recognised at either the political or social level. Yet corporations have considerable access to governments, and influence. Fisher and Lovell (2003) refer to the 1997 manifesto commitment of the incoming Labour Government to bring the concept of pluralism into company law reform and for the concept of stakeholding to supersede the shareholder as the primary focus of corporate activity. This fundamental change to UK corporations was, however, frustrated by political lobbying by corporate interests. The removal of the commitment to pluralism led to the resignation from the government appointed committee that was reviewing how to implement the manifesto commitment, by the finance director of *The Body Shop*. He described himself as a proponent of social and environmental responsibility and as a consequence he was not prepared to remain a member of the committee once the commitment to enlightened shareholder value had replaced pluralism. Newspaper reports on the outcome of the committee's work talked of frantic lobbying by business interests that ultimately led to not only the retention of shareholders' interests being the only one formally recognised at law, but also the conversion of the committee's proposals for compulsory statements on corporate issues, into proposals that would only be voluntary, or at the discretion of directors.

Hobbes, (see Pojman, 1998), held a pessimistic view of human nature, seeing people as essentially selfish and untrustworthy. Thus, Hobbes deemed that a sovereign power was necessary, to which people would owe allegiance. The relationship between the sovereign power and the citizen was, in a Hobbesian world, a subjugated one where a citizen was quite different from one that would be acceptable in the 21st century. However, if conferring citizenship status upon corporations concerns people because of their distrust of corporations to act in socially beneficial ways, then a Hobbesian notion of citizenship has some appeal, but much depends upon the constitution and the constituent parts of that sovereign power.

As societies have developed and the scope of governments has increased, the inability of citizens to become active participants is viewed as a weakness of modern democratic states. In modern societies, political citizenship is increasingly limited to periodic elections of political representatives, where even the relevance of these is being questioned. For example, in the 2001 general election in the UK, only 58% of those eligible to vote did so, the lowest turnout for many years. Further, in the UK, local elections and those for the European Union achieve even lower levels of elector participation where approximately two out of three people do not vote. Thus, when the term citizen is employed there is a need to be clear about the form of citizenship being discussed.

One of the most widely expressed concerns about modern corporations is that they have relatively unfettered authority, with only limited responsibilities such as to keep within the laws of the land. Thus, there is a need to be more specific about the forms and levels of participation in the operations of the state when the phrase corporate citizenship is employed. Given the significance of business organisations within democratic (as well as undemocratic) states, the presumption must be that the corporate citizenship assumed by its advocates reflects the acceptance of certain societal responsibilities, although whether it is envisaged that there will be an equal bestowing of citizens' rights on corporations is far from clear.

Contributions to the debate over corporate citizenship are growing and writers such as Amoore (2002); Andriof and McIntosh (2001); Birch (2001); Cohen (2001); Davenport and Llewellyn (2001); Dion, (2001); Escobar (1975); Gautschi and Jones (1987); Gunnemann (1975); McIntosh *et al.* (2003); Powers (1975); Windsor (2001); Waddock (2001); Wood and Logsdon (2001); and Zadek, (2001a and 2001b), have argued from different vantage points and perspectives over the feasibility and desirability of the concept of corporate citizenship.

The publication edited by Gunnemann is particularly interesting because it represents a series of accounts of the debates that took place during 'consultations' or discussions that were held under the aegis of the Council on Religion and International Affairs (CRIA) that considered the tensions inherent between nation states and trans-national corporations, with special reference to Latin America. The presentation by Charles Powers, discussed the debate that took place within his corporation over whether to allow ethical considerations to be weighed in decisions affecting their operations in Latin America. He made the important point that to ignore the ethical dimension to decisions by allowing the economics of a situation to 'speak for themselves' *was* an ethical decision. He argued that there was no such thing as a value-neutral decision, because one's choice of decision criterion or criteria was a value-based decision. To base a decision upon what was best for the shareholders was an ethical decision where the decision might not be ethically correct, but the basis of the criteria employed had ethical implications.

Whether corporations can assume the status of citizens, and if so, whether such a development is desirable, is a matter of debate and argument. Invariably factors that could seriously undermine such progress become evident. For example, the best case scenarios for locating corporations within socio-political structures contain those elements necessary for the complete subversion of socio-political systems by corporate interests. However, the worst-case scenario for the domination of socio-political systems by corporate interests can also hold the prospect for more active participation by the citizenry.

Essentially, the relationships between the societal, economic and political dimensions to human existence are dynamic where the role of the individual is an extremely minor, yet also an extremely critical, one. The concept of corporate citizenship will develop in relation to the force of the arguments, the actions of individuals and pressure groups and the practices of corporations. At their heart are ethical issues and choices.

Summary

On its own classifying the corporation as a citizen does not take the issue of CSR forward, as an adjective is needed, such as 'good' or 'responsible' for it to have a positive connotation. By attributing the status of citizenship to corporations it may be hoped that corporations will take on the mantel of responsibility that such a status should bestow (*eg* Donaldson and Freeman, 1994). However, normally citizenship confers rights as well as responsibilities and it is not clear which rights, if any, corporations should be allowed to exercise. The notion of a corporation is a dynamic one, but to avoid unintended consequences it is vital that concepts such as citizenship are carefully thought through before being bestowed, to avoid corporations assuming certain rights without adopting all the required responsibilities of citizenship.

CHAPTER NINE

GOVERNMENT-BUSINESS RELATIONSHIPS

One of the principal reasons for wishing to adopt a more holistic approach to the business-society relationship is that corporations wield, both potentially and actually, great influence over social and political systems and institutions. Notable examples exist where such power and influence have been used in ways that have given rise to great concern.

It is always possible to highlight acts by individual people or specific corporations that present a poor image of the groups that they are said to represent. Proverbially speaking, individual bad apples do not necessarily tell us much about the rest of the apples in a barrel. However, if one can point to trends, allegiances, purposeful manipulation of power by large corporations, or groups of corporations on a regular basis, then the issue may be something more than the odd bad apple. In addition, business in general has a vested interest in the maintenance of particular economic and legal conditions. As Cavanagh (1990) observed, private investors and MNCs that seek to invest overseas look for:

> ... political stability, local banks willing to lend, and a potential workforce that is willing and trainable. They prefer a society in which the government can guarantee law and order and a sympathetic environment. (p.20).

Dictatorships provide such conditions. Bonner (1987), using the Philippines as an example, referred to a comment made by a US Embassy officer:

Democracy is not the most important issue for US foreign policy in the Philippines, … more important was the US national interest, our security interest, and our economic interest. (Cavanagh, 1990, p.20).

Cavanagh (1990) provided further examples of American Government involvement in a range of Latin American countries, including Chile, Uruguay and Guatemala, as examples of countries that the US has helped to 'stabilise' by providing aid loans and other support to ensure that the governments remained sympathetic to American business and political interests.

As part of the pluralist political system, business organisations lobby governments and parliaments to achieve the conditions and laws that suit them. In the modern era it is argued that pressure groups, and particularly business pressure groups, have a far more significant influence upon the construction of legislation than the polity in general. Fisher and Lovell (2003) provide examples of both the involvement of business and governments in sordid human events, and the political influence of business corporations.

One of the major concerns of the big business-government relationship is the way that individual corporations and industry sectors buy favour via sponsorship in one form or another. The most obvious example relates to the donations made to American political parties. A study published in *The Guardian* newspaper, and reproduced in Fisher and Lovell (2003) shows the donations made by major industries to the Republican Party in the run-up to the 2001 presidential election, and the decisions taken by the new president within the first three months of him coming to office, which affected those industries that had been major donors to his campaign.

The most notable examples were those relating to oil and gas, pharmaceuticals and the tobacco industry. The oil and gas industry made donations totalling $25.4m to the Republican Party and within three months of assuming office President Bush's administration had scrapped the Kyoto accord on pollution controls and global warming; had abandoned previously agreed CO_2 emission controls; and opened the previously protected Arctic refuge for exploratory drilling. With respect to tobacco, the industry had donated $7m to the Republican Party and in return saw the removal of federal lawsuits against tobacco manufacturers. The pharmaceutical industry was a donor to the tune of $17.8m and it saw the removal of price controls on Medicare (the government supported health insurance), which had been planned by the previous Clinton administration. All these actions were effected within three months of President Bush taking office.

Oestreich (2002) took his analysis beyond the individual company and industry sector-to-business relationship by considering the impact of the stipulations imposed upon developing countries by the major inter-governmental organisations (IGOs), notably the International Monetary Fund (IMF), the World Bank and the World Trade Organisation (WTO), when new trade or financial arrangements were being negotiated. Oestreich observed that the 'adjustment' programmes of The World Bank and IMF, had forced:

> ... third world countries to cut government spending (including spending on education, health care and other social sectors) and to open themselves to foreign competition (rather than protecting domestic producers), [and had thus] exacerbated the poverty already widespread in the third world, [which] had led to social dislocation and ... rolled back progress in the social sphere. (p.209).

Yet WTO talks held in September 2003 to discuss and agree the removal of subsidies paid by *developing* countries, notably the United States and the European Union member states, to their food producers, broke down without agreement. The power of the multinational food producing corporations is considerable, and even on the domestic front their ability to exert political influence has been noted. Cavanagh (1990) cites examples of how the big (non-agricultural) corporations in America had moved into farming and swept up practically all the subsidies paid out to American 'farmers'. Whilst the legislation was passed with the ostensible remit of supporting small-scale American farmers - the archetypal 'settler' scraping a living from the land - the overwhelming proportion of the grants and subsidies went to the large land-owning corporations.

Oestreich (2002) acknowledged that the World Bank and IMF would claim that the economic strictures placed upon developing countries were inevitable due to most of the developing countries being bankrupt because of past economic mismanagement. What is missing from the Oestreich account is reference to the subsidies paid to food producers in the so-called developed world and the position of the World Bank and the IMF with respect to these subsidies.

Pilger (2001 and 2003) referred to this issue when discussing the aftermath of the fall of the western-government backed regime of President Suharto of Indonesia. Suharto had come to power in a bloody civil war in 1966. The civil war, with American involvement, was estimated to have cost around one million lives. An abbreviated account of the accession of Suharto and the way the natural resources of Indonesia were distributed amongst mainly American, but also UK and other European companies, is provided by Fisher and Lovell (2003).

Suharto resigned from office in 1998, in the midst of demonstrations against unemployment and other economic and social conditions, amidst allegations of having fraudulently misappropriated up to $10bn of World Bank funds (Pilger, 2001). However, following his resignation and with the economic turmoil that remained, the IMF offered the post-Suharto government a 'rescue package' of multi-million-dollar loans. However, there were conditions. These included the elimination of tariffs on staple foods. "Trade in all qualities of rice has been opened to general importers and exporters" (Pilger, 2001). Fertilisers and pesticides lost their 70% subsidy, thereby ending the prospects for many farmers for staying on their land. They too were forced to try and find work in the cities, which were already over-burdened with unemployed 'citizens' looking for work. However, "it gives the green light to the giant food grains corporations to move into Indonesia" (Pilger, 2001).

Indonesia has still to repay interest on the loans from the World Bank that it acknowledges it never received because they were misappropriated by Suharto. Amid this carnage one of the few groups to prosper are the multinational food exporters because the import tariffs and subsidies that existed in Indonesia have been removed, even though the subsidies received by the multinational food operators of America and the European Union from their governments remain. Notions of justice, equity and freedom are difficult to discern in such an example and raise the issue of the globalising effects of corporate business.

Globalisation

A number of the issues addressed in relation to corporate citizenship are applicable to any discussion of globalisation. However, there are certain elements of the globalisation debate that require more focused attention and are not associated with corporate citizenship or corporate social responsibility issues directly.

Employing a Rawlsian (1971) approach, it can be argued that the harm that corporations can do if they only meet the minimum constraints to their activities specified by law contradicts, in many cases, the difference principle, particularly given the power of large corporations to obtain legislation that suits their interests. An application of the Rawlsian original position test might cast doubt upon the efficacy, let alone the ethicality, of the poor being better-off as a result of MNC-globalisation and WTO strictures, rather than the employment of other, more culturally and socially sensitive approaches to economic development. The evidence that corporations lobby for 'business-friendly' conditions reinforces the view that corporations employ an ethical-egoist approach to their activities rather than the bounded/constrained self-interest approach of Adam Smith. Their perspective resembles far more one of societal members acting apart from society, rather than as a part of society.

Nearly 200 years ago, David Ricardo (Hutchinson, 1981) described profit as 'the lever and the lure'. The lure was because profit was an indicator of how successfully capital has been invested and thereby acted as a lure to new capital investment. The lever, related to the social, as well as the economic, impact that capital migration could have on whole communities. The migration of capital from one region to another, from one country to another, as it seeks out the most advantageous investment opportunities, can have a destabilising impact upon those areas affected by such capital flows. Whilst Friedman (1970) points to the undemocratic nature of corporate social responsibility, to leave business alone ignores the profound influence of corporate decisions, and their impact upon potentially millions of lives. Corporate decisions are made by unseen and largely unaccountable, decision makers. Critics of Friedman's 'undemocratic' argument see these issues as far more significant and serious threats to democratic processes, than those raised by Friedman.

A number of distinctive and useful contributions have been made to the phenomenon referred to as globalisation, and these include, Amoore (2002); Berenbeim (1999); De George (1993); Enderlie (1995); Enteman (2001); Gilpin (2002); Gunnemann (1975); Harvey (1994); Held (2002); Hutton (2002); Litvin (2003); McGrew (2002); O'Sullivan (2001); Rosenau (2002); Sell (2002); Soros (2000); Stiglitz (2002); and Woods (2002).

Oestreich (2002) made some interesting observations with regard to globalisation and its ethical justification. He acknowledged that a 'utilitarian calculus' offered a mechanism possessing some apparent (ethical) logic. The neo-classical economic justification of an unfettered market approach to stimulating economic development in 'late-developing-countries' (LDCs) was the most reliable way of providing the greatest good for the greatest number. It allowed people to determine their good. It was pointless, and counter-productive, to stand in the way of progress, or to try to guarantee that there were no 'losers' at all in international trade. The end result would be that a system that tried to avoid hurting anyone would at best be a stagnant one and at worst would collapse under the weight of its commitments.

This sort of utilitarianism has directness, a simplicity, an economic logic, which is appealing to development finance and business. But it is also a cruel philosophy in its willingness to ignore the suffering of some in the name of the welfare of others. The utilitarian sees development as a matter of increasing the GDP of developing countries. As GDP is the standard way of measuring economic well-being and utility more money in the macro economy means more satisfied citizens.

However, some would argue that the demands of justice *versus* efficiency go beyond the distribution of goods. Justice has powerful political overtones that are anathema to those concerned primarily with the logic of the market. To justify the approach outlined above the libertarian argument needs to decouple the economics from the politics, whereas those with concerns about globalisation would argue that the two are inextricably linked. Oestreich (2002) argues that trade deals are made by the elites to benefit themselves or their supporters. International business is conceived within a larger frame of political exploitation, where countries with less developed economies are 'managed' in order to benefit richer nations, which need them to provide cheap materials and goods.

Justice requires political intervention of a type which free-trade advocates find unacceptable. This is not just an intervention to help the poor and the vulnerable within society, but, Oestreich (2002) argues,

> ... *an effort to preserve cultures, to protect vulnerable groups, and to safeguard an environmental patrimony. In short, anti-globalization*

protestors recognize that in pursuit of justice there are many goods that
are just as important as material possessions, and that these too must
be controlled by politics if justice is to be approached. (p.216).

This is a bleak view of globalisation and ignores the serious efforts
that some corporations are making to wrestle with the challenges that
globalising their operations present. To present global corporations as
a homogenous group is simplistic and ignores the examples of good
practice that exist. The Levi-Strauss corporation is referred to in
chapter eleven both to provide evidence of some examples of good
practice, and to highlight some of the not-so-straight-forward ethical
situations that can abound. An example of such complex ethical issues
is the challenge facing MNCs as they strive to achieve consistency of
practice across their worldwide operations. The issues of promotion
based upon meritocracy rather than nepotism, the status of women,
the use of child labour, and other practices are each fraught with
tensions and cultural variations. This is not an argument for ethical
relativism, but rather a recognition that achieving universal minimum
standards of behaviour and respect is far from the simple issue it might
first appear.

However, notwithstanding such problems, there is evidence that
some (more than might be an acceptable number of) corporations see
the economies of LDCs as purely exploitative situations and that as soon
as conditions change in those LDCs, they, the multinational corporation,
will exit to the next profitable opportunity. Indeed, by definition if the
living conditions, employment conditions and employment legislation,
safety requirements, taxation laws and environmental controls were as
strict in LDCs as they are in western countries then multinational and
transnational corporations would have no production cost differential to
exploit. Cheap goods in the west are the result of lower than western-
standards of human and environmental protection and respect. The
'happiness' criterion of utilitarianism is expressed by way of movements

in GDP. The situation appears to demand a far more articulate, inclusive and representative expression of 'happiness'.

Just as it is over simplistic to bracket all MNCs and TNCs under one homogenous classification, so too is it overly simplistic to treat globalisation as if its effects have been consistent across the globe. As Stiglitz (2002) observes, globalisation has had a dramatic and positive effect in a number of countries and regions, notably parts of east Asia. Globalisation has brought better health, as well as an active global civil society fighting for more democracy and greater social justice (p.214).

However, Stiglitz (2002) also accepts that:

> ... *globalisation is not working for many of the world's poor* [and] *it is not working for much of the environment* [and] *it is not working for the stability of the global economy.* (p.214).

Stiglitz's remedy is for more effective management of the global economy, that is anathema to liberal free market advocates.

Interestingly, Hutton (2002), in his agenda for action, points to moves to force the individual stock markets of Europe to make their listing requirements fall in line with those in New York, and that European finance and trade ministers have come under intense pressure to enshrine in company law that the primacy and exclusive focus of corporations is the shareholder (as is already the case in the UK). In addition pressure has been exerted to make hostile takeovers and market-based financial engineering easier in the name of market efficiency. The 'pressure' has come from American interests and these changes are intended to facilitate a 'market for control'. Hutton congratulated the German ministers who vetoed these proposals, arguing that hostile takeovers tended to reduce value, rather than add value. No mention was made of the ethicality of the processes employed or the ramifications of the proposals, had they been accepted. Hutton argued that,

If the rest of the world is not careful, our future will be to accept globalization almost on American conservative terms and around American conservative preoccupations. (p.353).

This would mean individualism defined exclusively in terms of a 'consumer' and a form of freedom that was apart from society as distinct from a part of society (Bellah *et al*, 1985).

The future shape of globalisation is not predestined (Thomson, 2002; Sen, 1985, 1999; Williams, 1985). Hutton (2002) and Stiglitz (2000, 2002) offer a critical analysis of current institutional performance, but also consider ideas for a way forward.

Summary

The phenomenon known as globalisation presents new ethical and moral challenges to businesses and societies. Possibly at no other time has the need arisen, as it now does, for MNCs to try and achieve universal minimum standards of care and respect for people across the globe. Previously cultural variations were at least recognised, if not tolerated or found acceptable, with respect to employees and customers. Now, in order to reduce the risk of being seen to be exploitative of either elements within the supply chain or customers, and face adverse publicity with the attendant effects upon sales and profits, MNCs have to try and standardise practices around common, acceptable levels. This cannot be an easy task and is one reason for the claim at the start of chapter one that ethics in business opens up new areas of exploration for ethicists.

CHAPTER TEN

INTER-INSTITUTIONAL CODES OF ETHICS

As a way of establishing minimum levels of behaviour within their global operations, corporations tend to establish codes of ethics for their employees. Codes also operate between corporations and governments. Codes of conduct for MNCs can take various forms and the International Labour Office (ILO) cites three factors that tend to determine the credibility with which codes for MNCs are regarded:

(i)   the specific governments that have adopted and support the codes, and the particular MNCs that have 'signed-up' to the codes;

(ii) whether a code actually addresses the critical issues of the business activity being considered; and

(iii) the effectiveness of the monitoring mechanisms employed and the sanctions available.

The International Chamber of Commerce (ICC) is active in pursuing a self-regulatory framework for business operations on the world stage. It sets standards which recognise the tensions inherent within any competitive market setting. The following statement is drawn from one of the publications of the ICC, although obtained from an ILO website:

> *The globalisation of the world's economies, and the intense competition which ensues therefrom, require the international business community to adopt standard rules. The adoption of these self-disciplinary rules is the best way that business leaders have of demonstrating that they*

are motivated by a sense of social responsibility, particularly in light of the increased liberalization of markets.

(http://www.itcilo/english/actrav/telearn/global/ilo/guide/main.htm

A number of initiatives and codes have been developed to address specific global business issues:

- The 1990s saw some agreements expand to take in broader social issues. An example is the *Japan Federation of Economic Organisations*. Established in 1996 it covers a number of issues including philanthropic activities, resistance against organisations that undermine social cohesion, policies to enrich the lives of employees, safe and comfortable work environments, a respect for individual dignity and 'specialness', and corporate transparency.

- In 1996 the *British Toy and Hobby Association* developed a code of practice that forbids the use of forced, indentured or underage labour in the production of toys. The agreement also mentions the working and living conditions of employees. An amended form of this code was adopted by the *International Council of Toy Industries* later in 1996.

- In February 1997, the ILO, the Sialkot Chamber of Commerce (SCCI) in Pakistan and UNICEF formed an agreement to eliminate child labour in the production of footballs by 1999. This specific initiative was the result of worldwide publicity of the use of child labour in the production of footballs, although no other products or industries were specifically targeted. It appears that this initiative has been largely, if not completely successful. It appears that high-profile media coverage is conducive to, and possibly necessary for, change to be levered and achieved.

- In the US similar codes have been developed in relation to other industries. For example, *The Apparel Partnership on Sweatshops and Child Labour* which was adopted in 1997.

- The Organisation for Economic Cooperation and Development (OECD) has also produced guidelines for Multinational Enterprises covering labour relations.

- A variety of organisations have sponsored the *Sweatshop and Clean Clothes Codes,* which cover labour relations, health and safety issues, freedom of association, wages and benefits and hours of work.

- The *Declaration of Principles concerning Multinational Enterprises,* developed in 1997 and involving the ILO, is a code that addresses issues such as 'freedom of association', terms and conditions of work.

- An international standard was developed, known as Social Accountability 8000 (SA 8000) by the Council on Economic Priorities Accreditation Agency (CEPAA), a not-for-profit organisation. It is similar to other standards such as ISO 9000, which deals with quality assurance, and ISO 14000 that concerns environmental standards. The intention is that an organisation's social and ethical practices (including those of its suppliers) can be independently assessed against published standards and if the organisations pass the scrutiny they will be awarded a certificate or kite mark as evidence that they have reached appropriate standards.

Although a wide range of companies, governments and non-governmental organisations (NGOs) were consulted during the development of the SA 8000 standard, some NGOs concerned with international labour standards criticised CEPAA for being too close to the views of the large corporations. Nevertheless, the standard was an attempt to formalise universal ethical standards for businesses and organisations.

At first sight the existence of such codes presents a preferable state of affairs to that of no codes at all. However, a closer inspection of such codes poses some uncomfortable challenges to this assumption. For example, within the *Sweatshop Code*, the wording relating to 'wages and benefits' specifies:

> ... *employers shall pay employees, as a floor, at least the minimum wage required by local law or the prevailing industry wage, whichever is the higher, and shall provide legally mandated benefits.*

This leaves much of the responsibility with governments to institute laws that enhance working and employment conditions. The lobbying of governments by MNCs will clearly be a voice that will be listened to in LDC government circles. Those employed in sweatshop conditions are not often well-represented at the political negotiating table. In the meantime global organisations and Western customers of the manufacturing output of developing countries remain free to exploit the cost differentials of sourcing their production capacity overseas. Indeed, the very reason why many western apparel companies have closed their western production capability and transferred production to locations such as in the Philippines, India and Honduras, has been to exploit the cost advantage of the developing world, cost advantages that have often involved sweatshop conditions and child labour.

With regard to 'hours of work' the *Sweatshop code* states that:

> *Except in extraordinary business circumstances, employees shall: (i) not be required to work more than the lesser of (a) 48 hours per week and 12 hours overtime or (b) the limits on regular and overtime hours allowed by the law of the country of manufacture or, where the laws of such country do not limit the hours of work, the regular work week in such country plus 12 hours overtime; and (ii) be entitled to at least one day off in every seven day period.*

Thus, unless local laws state otherwise, employers can require their workers to work 60 hours per week and stay within the obligations of the code. Employees might be entitled to one day off per week, but whether they will get this is another matter. In addition, when demand is high, the working week can extend beyond the 60 hours. This should be constrained to 'extraordinary business circumstances', but the latter is not defined and less than scrupulous employers will use this as a loophole to work employees for all 7 days of the week and exceed the 60 hours per employee. The code could be far more stringent in its demands on behalf of the employees (the majority of whom tend to be women), but of course, the closer wage rates and working conditions are pushed towards western levels, the less the original decision to source production to the developing country makes economic sense.

There are examples of organisations appearing to make serious efforts to put their codes into practice. The ILO reported that Levi-Strauss, for example, conducted annual global training programmes to ensure that its audit managers were familiar with their internal code, and had conducted five-day training programmes in the Dominican Republic for 'terms of engagement' auditors. Liz Claiborne (an American retail organisation of women's fashion clothes) had also reported that it had intensified its efforts to identify and remove labour abuses.

The rigour with which MNCs police their own codes of conduct (particularly those they apply to their suppliers) appears to vary. Of Liz Claiborne, the plant manager of *Primo Industries*, an apparel contractor based in El Salvador, stated, "they are the toughest on child labour". The plant manager told US Department of Labour officials that inspectors from Liz Claiborne visited the plant 'approximately twice a month to check on quality control and see whether rules and regulations are being implemented'. Such vigilance by the Claiborne organisation must involve the incurrence of costs that some other organisations (maybe its competitors) do not appear to incur, at least not to the same extent. A manager with the Indian company, *Zoro Garments*, 75% of whose output goes to US markets, is quoted as saying that:

> ... *representatives of US customers have visited Zoro's factory occasionally for quality control inspections,* [but] *most of the visits were walk-throughs with some general questions raised about the use of child labour, but no check-list of requirements was administered.* http://www.itcilo/english/actrav/telearn/global/ilo/guide/ main.htm

A complicating issue is where a MNC sources products from a variety of overseas suppliers, with some of these suppliers being in monopsony relationships with the MNC, whilst for other suppliers the MNC in question might be only one amongst a range of customers. Thus, can a MNC be held responsible for a supplier's work conditions and labour practices from which it sources relatively few orders? Whatever one's position on this question, it has to be taken for granted that, for production costs of suppliers from developing countries to be so much lower than their western competitors, wage rates and employment conditions cannot be equal. Thus, for MNCs, or any other form of organisation, to feign ignorance of the working conditions of some of its suppliers ignores the logic of the situation. One approach is that rather than assuming that all is satisfactory, the cost differentials between suppliers of developing and developed countries would suggest a default position that all is not satisfactory, and that evidence is required to disprove this assumption.

Establishing a corporate code of conduct is one thing, making it a part of everyday practice is another. Of the 42 apparel companies surveyed by the US Department of Labor in 1996, to establish how many of them had endeavoured to ensure that workers in their overseas suppliers were aware of their code of conduct, "very few respondents indicated that they had tried". Only three companies insisted on their codes being posted onto their suppliers' notice boards. In a further study reported by the ILO, of 70 supplier companies, 23 (33%) indicated that they were not aware of corporate codes of conduct issued by their US customers.

The US Department of Labour also undertakes company visits and the ILO website gives information on their visits to a variety of countries including El Salvador, the Dominican Republic, Honduras, India and the Philippines. In a study of 70 companies, managers at only 47 of these stated an awareness of such codes, and of these only 34 could produce a copy of a code. Thus, less than half of the sites visited could produce a principal customer's code, yet the US retailers refer to their supplier codes as evidence of their (the apparel retailers') commitment to ethical practices at their overseas suppliers.

Awareness of such codes was highest in El Salvador, where managers at six out of the nine companies visited were aware of such codes, whereas in India managers at only two of the seven producer sites visited were aware. Even where awareness was acknowledged, awareness was not the same as accepting the codes and adhering to them. As the ILO observed:

> ... although a significant number of suppliers knew about the US corporate codes of conduct, meetings with workers and their representatives in the countries visited suggested that relatively few workers were aware of the existence of codes of conduct, and even fewer understood their implications.

Carasco and Singh (2003) argue that transnational corporate codes of ethics, in establishing global ethics, have the potential to succeed where inter-governmental organisations have failed. However, Kolk *et al.* (1999); Kolk and Tulder (2002); McDonald and Nijhof (1999); and Prakash (2000) challenge both this assumption and the performance of TNCs and MNCs in establishing and living up to such codes.

The above portrays a picture of some good practice, but raises the concern that the general picture is far from satisfactory. It is instructive to bring to bear on the situation some of the ideas and concepts discussed in part A of this review. For example:

- Would the current state of affairs between LDCs and the major players in the WTO be the likely outcome if all of the representatives at the WTO went behind Rawls' veil of ignorance?

- What are the principal virtues that explain the current ability of American and European Union member states' governments to negotiate the removal of agricultural subsidies from LDCs, but to retain the subsidies they pay to their own food producers?

- Does the transfer of production capacity to a country with low environmental controls, lax safety standards, and poor employment conditions for workers, with an attendant rise in the profits of the MNC concerned, reflect exceptional business acumen on the part of the MNC's senior executives and thereby represent appropriate grounds for large increases in executive pay?

The UN Global Compact

A potentially significant step to engage MNCs in addressing global issues beyond the economic happened in 1999 when the UN established the UN Global Compact. Frustrated by the lack of progress of governments to respond adequately to addressing issues such as child labour and inhuman working conditions in companies located in the developing economies, but which were part of the supply chains of large international organisations, the United Nations set-up the UN Global Compact. In the words of Global Compact's Chief Executive, the Global Compact was established to fill a void, to "respond to demands and needs that governments were either unwilling or unable to meet" (Kell, 2004).

The Compact was, and remains, a voluntary code that is intended to influence corporate practices by:

(i) gaining the support and membership of leading organisations; and

(ii) increasing the acceptance and take-up of corporate responsibility by disseminating examples of good practice that hopefully other organisations will adopt.

The Compact focuses upon nine key principles of corporate activity, which are grouped into three categories.

Human rights

Principle 1   Businesses are asked to support the protection of international human rights within their sphere of influence; and

Principle 2   To ensure their own corporations are not complicit in human rights abuses.

Labour

Principle 3   Businesses are asked to uphold the freedom of association and the effective recognition of the rights to collective bargaining;

Principle 4   To eliminate all forms of forced and compulsory labour;

Principle 5   To abolish child labour; and

Principle 6   To help eliminate discrimination in respect of employment and occupation.

Environment

Principle 7   Businesses are asked to support a precautionary approach to environmental challenges;

Principle 8   To undertake initiatives to promote greater environmental responsibility; and

Principle 9   To encourage the development and diffusion of environmentally friendly technologies.

In 1999 those responsible for the Compact saw the future for social change to be through international corporations, hence the focus on working with significant organisations to both gain their support (patronage) and stimulate corporate responsibility (CR) by highlighting examples of good practice that 'work' and that could be seen to be compatible with being a successful company.

The Foreword to the 2004 report *Gearing Up*, which was commissioned by the executive of *Global Compact*, reflects a development in this thinking and strategy. There now appears to be a recognition that it was unrealistic to expect corporations to respond to initiatives such as the Global Compact independent of governments. Whilst the original Global Compact may have been a response to political failings, a voluntary initiative that asks businesses to make good the failings of governments, ironically, needs the commitment and positive engagement of governments to help it develop. For this reason *Gearing Up* argues for a greater level of dialogue, collaboration and partnership between businesses and governments for the future development of corporate responsibility.

A key aim of *Gearing Up* is stated as making "the link between corporate responsibility (CR) initiatives and wider sustainable development challenges", with the report linked to the Millennium Development Goals (MDGs).

THE MILLENNIUM DEVELOPMENT GOALS

1   Eradicate extreme poverty and hunger

2   Achieve universal primary education

3   Promote gender equality and empower women

4   Reduce child mortality

5   Improve maternal health

6   Combat HIV/AIDS, malaria and other diseases

7   Ensure environmental sustainability, and

8   Develop a global partnership for development (this relates to trade issues, but also debt relief and access to affordable, essential drugs in developing countries).

Summary

The codes that have been introduced to address the many issues relating to the operation of MNCs are invariably voluntary, including the UN Global Compact. Some of these codes have not included corporate contributions, either through choice or because of differences of view, but many operate as reference points for NGOs and government bodies.

The UN Global Compact began life as an instrument to tackle the world's 'wicked' problems (a term used in the late 1990s to describe the perennial, knotty, national, social problems in the UK). It has since been recognised that such an approach was unrealistic and that, with all their faults, national and super-national governments have to be part of the concerted effort required to tackle the world's great problems that are reflected in the Millennium Development Goals.

A way forward from this apparent morass of complex and competing ethical perspectives is required. No panaceas are available, but if movement is to be achieved a framework must be developed that allows flexibility within minimum and universalisable set of standards of behaviour. Integrative Social Contract Theory (ISCT) is possibly the most robust framework currently being debated by ethicists and is considered in the next chapter.

CHAPTER ELEVEN

SOCIAL CONTRACT THEORY AND ITS POSSIBILITIES

The concept of a social contract is rooted in political theory. Its source can be traced back to Plato (1935), Bosanquet (1906) and Aristotle (Allan, 1970), but more recently to Hobbes (1968), Locke (1952) and Rousseau (1913). Lessnoff (1986) provides a good introduction to the history of social contract. More recently, social contract theory has been taken up by those who argue that the concept has relevance beyond the relationship between the individual and the state, which is the focus of political theory. Its more recent articulation is found in the argument that corporations have to earn and maintain a 'license to operate'. The most notable writers working in this area are Donaldson (1982, 1989, 1990, 1996); Donaldson and Dunfee (1994, 1995 and 1999); Dunfee (1991, 1996); and Dunfee and Donaldson (1995). Donaldson and Dunfee have taken the social contract and developed a distinctive approach that they call *Integrative Social Contract Theory* (ISCT). At the core of the theory are four norms, or categories of values:

Hypernorms

These are fundamental human rights or basic prescriptions common to most religions. The values they represent are by definition acceptable to all cultures and all organisations. These have the characteristics of universal norms and are few in number. What is and is not a hypernorm would be agreed by rational debate, and any contender for 'hypernorm' status would fall if it could be shown to be unable to be universalised. This raises all the problems that Kantian ethics encounters, but rather than turning to something akin to Ross' (1930) *prima facie obligations* Donaldson and Dunfee introduce two 'lower level' norms that allow for 'local' variations to be possible. The first of these is *'consistent norms'*.

Consistent norms

These values are more culturally specific than hypernorms, but they will be consistent with hypernorms and other legitimate norms (the latter being defined as a norm that does not contradict the hypernorm screen, Donaldson and Dunfee, 1999). Donaldson and Dunfee cite corporate mission statements as examples of 'consistent norms'.

Moral free space

These are norms that might be in tension (or limited contradiction) with any of the hypernorms. An example of such a tension could be the use of child labour. Donaldson and Dunfee cite two examples involving the company Levi-Strauss. In the first example Levi-Strauss severed its links with the Tan family (and their businesses) because they (the Tan family) reportedly "held twelve hundred Chinese and Philippine women in guarded compounds working them seventy-four hours a week" (Franklin Research and Development Corporation, 1992). These practices contravened Levi-Strauss' Business Partners Terms of Engagement. The actions of the Tan family could be said to have contravened the hypernorms of respect for human dignity and justice.

The second example relates to the reaction of Levi-Strauss when it became aware that two of its suppliers in Bangladesh were employing children under the age of fourteen (a generally internationally accepted minimum age of employment). The company did not sever its relationship with the suppliers but chose an alternative course of action. The company required that the children be sent to school, with Levi-Strauss paying the children's tuition and associated fees, but also paying the children's wages to their families, so the latter did not suffer, but only while the children were at school. The company also agreed to re-employ the children when they reached fourteen. Whilst the exploitation of children was addressed by the hypernorms, ISCT also coped with the recognition of a locally 'accepted' practice, something that might, for the time being, be seen to reside within the 'moral free space'. This is not to say that for all companies the 'right' action would be to react as Levi-Strauss had. For some the use of children under the age of fourteen may have meant a severing of links with the suppliers concerned, irrespective of the ripple effects of this action. In this case one or more of the hypernorms would not allow the inclusion of the use of children less than fourteen years of age within the moral free space, notwithstanding that it was an 'accepted' local norm. ISCT allows both of these (re)actions because of the relationship of 'moral free space' to 'hypernorms' and 'consistent norms'.

The final category is that of *illegitimate norms*: These norms are irreconcilable with *hypernorms*. For some this might be the case with regard to the treatment of women and children in some societies, but for others some of these 'problems' might fit within a 'moral free space' that would allow some development of understanding of all sides to see if a longer term relationship might be possible with some modification to the 'problems' in question. In this form of application, *moral free space* becomes something of a utilitarian concept, but only on the understanding that the intention is to achieve a longer-term correction of the offending practice and to do this most effectively it is better to work at the offending practice and to achieve change. In this way principled-based *hypernorms* can be overridden (in the short-term at least) by utilitarian considerations located within the *moral free space*.

As a result of the above type of example, ISCT has been criticised for being relativist. Donaldson and Dunfee refute this, arguing that ISCT is pluralist, combining universal norms of behaviour (hypernorms) with the recognition of important cultural differences (consistent norms and moral free space). The authors also recognise that within the theory, individuals, corporations and communities have to work out for themselves what are their respective 'norms', at all levels.

> *Business ethics should be viewed more as a story in the process of being written than as a moral code like the Ten Commandments. It can, and should ... adjust over time – to evolving technology, and to the cultural or religious attitudes of particular economic conditions.* (p.viii).

Donaldson and Dunfee go on to say,

> *At the heart of social contract effort is a simple assumption, namely that we can understand better the obligations of key social institutions, such as business or government, by attempting to understand what is entailed in a fair agreement or 'contract' between those institutions and society and also in the implicit contracts that exist among different communities and institutions within society. The normative authority of any social contract derives from the assumption that humans, acting rationally, consent – or at least would consent hypothetically – to the terms of a particular agreement affecting the society or community of which they are a member. In this manner contractarian theories utilise the device of consent, albeit it is often hypothetical consent, to justify principles, policies and structures.* (pp.16-17).

In order to provide a mechanism that might help operationalise ISCT, Donaldson and Dunfee employ a modified form of Rawls' veil of ignorance. Unlike Rawls' conception of the veil of ignorance, in which those (metaphorically) placed behind the veil have no knowledge of any aspect of their status, ethic origin, physical abilities, gender, geographic location, political and economic system, in Donaldson and Dunfee's conception only those aspects of a person's identity which are economic in nature, such as the level of personal skill, nature of economic system, type of employing organisation, employment position held, are concealed. This modified Rawlsian artifice facilitates a reflection and debate about an 'objective' fairness that should be inherent within an economic system and the ethical and moral base of that system.

ISCT attempts to hold on to both the integrity of universalisable norms (minimum accepted standards of behaviour irrespective of where in the world the norms are being considered), but avoid the inflexibility of non-consequentialist stances. This is addressed by the introduction of consistent norms and the moral free space. It is an interesting development, providing as it does a schema or framework that business people can employ to interrogate the ethical and moral issues that might be at stake in a particular situation.

Summary

Donaldson and Dunfee are emphatic that ISCT is not a framework, let alone approach, that can be employed unthinkingly. By its very nature it is a framework to facilitate discussion, debate and argument. It is not a decision-making tool, for the type of ethically charged situations that corporations are often faced with are invariably too complex and multi-faceted to lend themselves to an easy formulation and calculation. However, the ideas and categories within ISCT provide a language and a set of concepts that may help parties to a decision think constructively about the different issues and dimensions inherent within a complex business scenario.

CHAPTER TWELVE

CONCLUSION

Attempts to introduce a focus upon ethical dimensions to business activity within business educational programmes have, in the past, often been met with askance looks and questions about their relevance. From an academic point of view, one of the dramatic effects of globalisation has been to both raise the profile of ethical issues in business, but also to raise new ethical challenges, particularly those relating to universal norms in MNCs whose operational units are located in distinctive cultural and moral climates. Globalisation, and the demonstrations against individual companies and at inter-governmental meetings, have provided the evidence that a business strategy, either at the individual corporate level, the industry level, or the inter-governmental level, has not been developed from a clearly articulated ethical base, and that a collection of words on paper is likely to encounter profound resistance in one form or another. Paradoxically, the amoral claims that are sometimes made on behalf of business have, in the shape of globalisation, focused the debate upon ethics in business as no other phenomenon has done.

Part A of this review initially considered the developing field of 'business ethics' and the literature sources that have, and continue, to sustain its development. Beginning from around the 1920s, the role and place of 'the market' and 'the individual' have been central concepts together with the critical evaluation of the competing claims relating to the ethical base of business. Values and virtues have changed through time, reflecting the changes in discourse that shape an understanding of ethics. 'Work', once looked down upon in the time of Aristotle, had, by the mid-late seventeenth century, assumed the status of 'God's work on earth', at least in certain parts of the world. Chapter four reflected upon the thirteen virtues articulated by Benjamin Franklin, many of which appear to reflect a fundamental shift from the ethical underpinnings of Platonic and Aristotelian virtues. The primacy of the economy and work over the polity was evident, and an elective affinity cited by Weber between capitalism and Protestantism was seen as a useful mechanism with which to justify this change.

This literature review has drawn heavily upon American contributions and the travails of modern western capitalist societies for two related reasons. First, the American economy is the primary world economy and American influence at corporate, industry and governmental level is pre-eminent. As Hutton (2002) has observed, "the US has emerged as the globe's hyperpower". Secondly, as the engine of the world economy, the experiences of America pre-date those of the rest of the world and as a result the 'business ethics' literature is far more developed in America, although from a very particular, individualistic perspective. An appreciation of European contributions, over millennia, to philosophical issues and philosophical traditions, is often missing from American contributions.

The chapters in Part B of the review focus upon contemporary issues of how the business-society relationship can be developed. The issues of corporate social responsibility, the stakeholder perspective, the corporation as citizen, inter-institutional codes of ethics, and Integrative Social Contract Theory were all considered.

The challenges of the phenomenon described as globalisation are considerable, linked as they are to geo-political issues. The significance of the business ethics debate cannot be overestimated and the status of business ethics as a serious and distinguishable element of the broad field of 'Ethics' has the potential to make contributions to knowledge and understanding. Donaldson and Dunfee's development of social contract theory, the origins of which can be traced back to Plato, is an example.

The vista before business ethicists and business practitioners alike is rich, complex and challenging. There is a critical need for both to begin debating the issues together rather than at one another.

A two-way social contract?

What every sustainability and corporate responsibility initiative has to recognise and accept is that business corporations, in the form of their chief executives, have to be competitive in their respective market places. Until consumers not only express a wish for corporations to move beyond legal minima, but are prepared, in certain cases, to pay slightly higher prices for products or services produced and delivered in ways that are less harmful or more socially or environmentally sensitive than rival products, then corporate executives will feel that there is too much hypocrisy and double standards in many of the corporate responsibility debates. The social contract, which was discussed in chapter eight, tends to be presented as a one-way contract, that is, the conditions within the contract are placed exclusively upon corporations to maintain their (theoretical) 'license to operate'. But the demands of global environmental and social issues, as articulated in the *Global Compact,* suggest that a two-way social contract is more applicable.

The transfer of production capacity to less-developed economies is not only a reflection of capitalists seeking out the most profitable investment opportunities, but it is also evidence of the perpetual downward pressure on prices. The 'real' (inflation adjusted) cost of many products has been, and continues, downwards. For most customers, assuming the quality differential is not too marked, then price is the critical purchase criterion. Corporate executives need reassurance that, assuming any price differential between their own products and those of their competitors can be explained by the more environmental or socially-sensitive policies of their organisation, then consumers will respect this and not prejudice the more sustainable policies of the company by switching their purchasing allegiance to companies with lower prices, but less sustainable policies. In this respect governments have a potentially important part to play in either rewarding companies that operate with leading-edge environmental and social policies, or penalising those that do not. Such an approach might be anathema to market fundamentalists, but 'the market' (or more particularly 'the consumer') is too capricious and fickle a coordinating mechanism in these circumstances to be seen as the principal tool for resource allocation.

Thus, if corporations change their policies and practices to reflect more sustainable policies and practices, is there not a responsibility on the part of consumers, communities and societies to support them? This may mean higher prices in many situations, but governments have a potentially vital role to play in such scenarios by equalising prices using taxation policies and investment incentives. These issues reflect the profoundly important debate that needs to be increasingly part of political and social agendas.

REFERENCES

Abeng, T (1997), 'Business ethics in Islamic context: Perspectives of a Muslim business leader', *Business Ethics Quarterly*, Vol.7(3), pp.47-54.

Accounting Standards Steering Committee (1975), *The Corporate Report*.

Ackerman, R W (1975), *The Social Challenge to Business*, Harvard Press.

Acton, H (1970), *Kant's Moral Philisophy*, MacMillan.

Alhabshi, S O and A H Ghazali (1997), *Islamic Values and Management*, Institute of Islamic Understanding, Kuala Lumpur.

Allan, D J (1970), *The Philosophy of Aristotle*, Oxford University Press.

Amoore, L (2002), *Globalisation Contested: An international political economy of work*, Manchester University Press, Manchester.

Androif, H (2001), 'Patterns of stakeholder Partnership building', in Andriof J and M McIntosh (eds.), *Perspectives on Corporate Citizenship*, Greenleaf Publishing Limited.

Andriof J and M McIntosh (eds.) (2001), *Perspectives on Corporate Citizenship*, Greenleaf Publishing Limited.

Aranya, N (1984), 'The Influence of Pressure Groups on Financial Statements in Britain', in Lee, T A & R H Parker (eds.), *The Evolution of Corporate Financial Reporting*, pp.265-274, Garland Publishing Inc. New York & London.

Aristotle (1976), *The Ethics of Aristotle*, J A K Thompson, Penguin, Harmondsworth.

Arora, B (2002), *Critical dimensions of corporate citizenship*, Palgrave, Basingstoke.

Arrow, K J and L Hurwicz (1977), *Studies in Resource Allocation Processes*, Cambridge University Press, Cambridge.

Ayer, A J (1981), *Hume*, Oxford University Press.

Bauman, Z (1994), *Alone Again: Ethics after Certainty*, Demos.

Baumol, W J (1958), *The Moral Basis of a Backward Society*, The Free Press, Glencoe, Ill.

Baumol, W J (1975), 'Business Responsibility and Economic Behaviour', in E S Phelps *Altruism, Morality and Economic Theory*, (ed.), Sage Foundation, New York.

Baydoun, N and R Willett (2000), 'Islamic Corporate Reports', *Abacus*, Vol. 36, Issue 1.

Beck, L-W (1965), *A Commentary on Kant's Critique of Pure Reason*, University of Chicago.

Beesley, M E (1974), 'The Context of Social Responsibility in Business', in Beesley, M E (ed), *Productivity and Amenity: Achieving a Social Balance*, Croom Helm, London.

Beesley, M E and T Evans (1978), *Corporate Social Responsibility: A Reassessment*, Croom Helm, London.

Belal, A R (2002), 'Stakeholder accountability or stakeholder management: a review of UK firms' social and ethical accounting, auditing and reporting (SEAAR) practices', *Corporate Social Responsibility and Environmental Management*, Vol.9, pp.8-25

Bellah, R, R Madsen, W M Sullivan, A Swidler and S M Tipton (1985), *Habits of the Heart: Middle America Observed*, Hutchinson Education, London.

Bentham, J (1994), 'The Commonplace Book', in *The Works of Jeremy Bentham*, Vol.X, wd. J Bowring, Thoemnes Press, Bristol. Original edition (1843), Tait, Edinburgh.

Bentham, J (1982), *An Introduction tot the Principles of Morals and Legislation*, eds. Burns, J H and H L A Hart, Methuen, original edition 1781, London.

Berenbeim, R (1999), 'The Divergence of a Global Economy: One Company, One market, One Code, One world', *Vital Speeches of the Day*, Vol.65, p.22.

Berle, A and G Means (1932), *The Modern Corporation and Private Property*, Macmillan, New York.

Berle, A A (1958), *Economic Power and the Free Society*, Fund for the Republic, New York.

Berlin, I (1999), *The First and the Last*, Granta Books, London.

Berlin, I (1969), *Four Essays on Liberty*, Oxford University Press, London.

Besser, T L (2002), *The Conscience of capitalism*, Praeger, Westport, Connecticut.

BIM (British Institute of Management), (1974), 'The British Public Company: Its Role, Responsibilities and Accountability', Occasional Paper – New eries OPN 12, British Institute of Management, London.

Birch, D (2001), *Corporate Citizenship: rethinking business beyond corporate social responsibility*, in (eds.) Andriof J and M McIntosh, *Perspectives on Corporate Citizenship*, Greenleaf Publishing Limited.

Bloom, A (1987), *The Closing of the American Mind*, Simon & Schuster, New York.

Bonner, R (1987), *Waltzing with a Dictator: The Marcoses and the Making of American Policy*, Times Books, New York.

Boatright, S A and M J Naughton (eds.) (2002), *Rethinking the Purpose of Business: Interdisciplinary Essays from the Catholic Social Tradition*, University of Notre Dame Press, Notre Dame, Indiana.

Bosanquet, B (1906), A Companion to Plato's Republic, Rivingtons, London.

Bowie, N E (1999), *Business Ethics: A Kantian Perspective*, Blackwell Publishers, Mass.

Bowie, N E (1986), 'Business Ethics', in eds. DeMarco, J P and R M Fox, *New Directions in Ethics*, Routledge and Kegan Paul.

Bowles, S and R Edwards (1985), *Understanding Capitalism: Competition, Command and Change in the US Economy*, Harper & Row.

Braverman, H (1974), *Labor and Monopoly Capital: The Degradation of Work in the Twentieth Century*, Monthly Review Press, New York.

Breidlid, A, F C Brogger, O T Gulliksen and T Sirevag (eds.) (1996), *American Culture: An Anthology of Civilization Texts*, Routledge, London.

Brockman, J (1995), *The Third Culture: Beyond the Scientific Revolution*, Simon & Schuster.

Brown, J and P Duguid (2000), *The Social Life of Information*, Harvard Business School Press, Boston.

Buchholz, R A and S B Rosenthal (1998), *Business Ethics: The Pragmatic Path Beyond Principles to Process*, Prentice Hall.

Buckle, H T (1861), *History of Civilisation in England*, (no publisher given), London.

Buckley, S L (1998), *Usury Friendly? The Ethics of Moneylending – A Biblical Interpretation*, Grove Books, Cambridge.

Calkins, M S J (2000), 'Recovering Religion's Prophetic Voice for Business Ethics', *Journal of Business Ethics*, Vol.23, pp.339-352.

Calvez, J-Y and M J Naughton (2002), 'Catholic Social Teaching and the Purpose of Business Organization: A Developing Tradition', in (eds.) Cortright, S A and M J Naughton (2002), *Rethinking the Purpose of Business*, p.ix-xii, University of Notre Dame, Indiana.

Caputo, J D (1993), *Against Ethics*, Indiana University Press, Bloomington.

Carasco, E F and J B Singh (2003), 'The Content and Focus of the Codes of Ethics of the world's Largest Transnational Corporations', *Business and Society Review*, Vol.108, pp.71-94.

Carey, J L (1984), 'The Origins of Financial Reporting', in Lee, T A & R H Parker, (1984), (eds.) *The Evolution of Corporate Financial Reporting'*, pp.241-264, Garland Publishing Inc. New York & London.

Carlen, C (ed.) (1981), *The Papal Encyclicals,* Vol. II, McGrath Publishing Co.

Carr, A (1968), 'Is Business Bluffing Ethically', *Harvard Business Review*, Vol.46, January/February, pp.145-146, 148.

Carroll, A B (1998), 'The four faces of corporate citizenship', *Business and Society Review*, Vol.100, No.1, pp.1-7.

Carroll, A B (1991), 'The pyramid of corporate social responsibility: toward the moral management of organizational stakeholders', *Business Horizons*, July-Aug, pp.39-48.

Carroll, A B (1979), 'A three dimensional model of corporate social performance', *Academy of management review*, Vol.4, pp.497-505.

Carroll, A B and A K Buchholtz (2000), *Business and Society: Ethics and Stakeholder management*, 4th ed. South-Western College, Cincinnati.

Castro, B (1996), *Business & Society: A Reader in the History, Sociology and Ethics of Business*, Oxford University Press, New York.

CBI (Confederation of British Industry) (1973), *The Responsibility of the British Public Company*.

Cavanagh, G F (1990), *American Business Values*, 3rd ed. Prentice-Hall Inc, Englewood Cliffs.

Chandler, A D (1996), 'The Role of Business in the United States: A Historical, in (ed.), Castro, B (1996), *Business & Society: A Reader in the History, Sociology and Ethics of Business*, pp.60-68, Oxford University Press, New York.

Cheffins, B R (2001), 'History and the Global Corporate Governance Revolution: The UK Perspective', *Business History*, Vol.43, No.4, pp.87-118.

Chewning, R C (1984), 'Can Free Enterprise Survive Ethical Schizophrenia?', *Business Horizons*, March-April, pp.5-11.

Childs, J M (1997), 'Lutheran perspectives on ethical business in an age of downsizing', *Business Ethics Quarterly*, Vol.7(2), pp.123-31.

Clarkson, M B E (1994), *A risk based model of stakeholder theory*, Proceedings of the Toronto Conference on Stakeholder Theory. Centre for Corporate Social Performance and Ethics, University of Toronto, Toronto, Canada.

Clarkson, M B E (1995), 'A stakeholder framework for analyzing and evaluating corporate social performance', *Academy of Management Review*, Vol.20(1), pp.92-117.

Coates, A W (ed.) (1971), *The Classical Economists and Economic Policy*, Methuen, London.

Cohen, J (2001), 'the world's business; the United Nations and the globalisation of corporate citizenship', in Andriof J and M McIntosh (eds.) (2001), *Perspectives on Corporate Citizenship*, Greenleaf Publishing Limited.

Cortright, S A and M J Naughton (2002), *Rethinking the Purpose of Business*, University of Notre Dame, Indiana.

Cowe, R (2001), 'Europe rises to social challenge: Corporate Citizenship, *Financial* Times, 19 July.

Crane, A and D Matten (2004), *Business Ethics: A European Perspective,* Oxford University Press.

Crouch, C and D Marquand (eds.) (1993), *Ethics and Markets: Co-operation and competition within capitalist economies*, Blackwell Publishers.

Daly, H E (1991), *Steady State Economics*, 2nd edition, Island Press, Washington, DC.

Daly, H E and J B J Cobb (1989), *For the Common Good: Redirecting the Economic towards Community, the Environment ad a Sustainable Future,* Beacon Press, Boston.

Davenport, K S and P Lewellyn (2001), 'Corporate citizenship: What gets recorded/ What gets rewarded?' in Andriof J and M McIntosh, (eds.) (2001), *Perspectives on Corporate Citizenship*, Greenleaf Publishing Limited.

Dawkins, R (2003), *A Devil's Chaplain: Selected essays by Richard Dawkins*, Weidenfeld & Nicolson.

Dawkins, R (1988), *The Blind Watchmaker*, Penguin Books.

De George, R T (1993), *Competing with Integrity in International Business,* Oxford University Press, New York.

De George, R T (1987), 'The Status of Business Ethics: Past and Future', *Journal of Business Ethics*, Vol.6, pp.201-211.

De George, R T (1982), 'What is the American value System?', *Journal of Business Ethics*, November.

Denhardt, R B (1981), *In the Shadow of the Organisation*, Regents Press, Lawrence KS.

Dion, M (2001), 'Corporate citizenship as an ethic of care; corporate values, codes of ethics and global governance', in Andriof J and M McIntosh (eds.) (2001), *Perspectives on Corporate Citizenship*, Greenleaf Publishing Limited.

Domini, A L and P D Kinder (1982), *Ethical Investing*, Addison-Wesley Publishing Co.

Donaldson, T (1996), 'Values in tension: Ethics away from home', *Harvard Business Review*, Vol.74(5), pp.48-56.

Donaldson, T (1990), 'Morally privileged relationships', *Journal of Value Enquiry*, Vol.24, pp.1-15.

Donaldson, T (1989), *The ethics of international business*, Oxford University Press, New York.

Donaldson, T (1982), *Corporations and Morality*, Prentice Hall, Englewood Cliffs, NJ.

Donaldson, T and T W Dunfee (1999), *Ties That Bind: A Social Contracts Approach to Business Ethics*, Harvard Business School Press, Boston, Massachusetts.

Donaldson, T and T W Dunfee (1995), 'Integrative social contracts theory: A commutarian conception of economic ethics', *Economics and Philosophy*, Vol.11(1), pp.85-112.

Donaldson, T and T W Dunfee (1994), 'Toward a unified conception of of business ethics: Integrative social contracts theory', *Academy of Management Review*, Vol.19(2), pp.252-284.

Donaldson, T and P H Werhane (1979), *Ethical Issues in Business: A Philosophical Approach*, Prentice Hall, New Jersey.

Donaldson, T J and R E Freeman (eds.) (1994), *Business as a Humanity*, Oxford University Press, New York.

Donner, W (1991), *The Liberal Self: John Stuart Mill's Moral and Political Philosophy*, Cornell University Press.

Dorff, E N (1997), 'The implications of Judaism for business and privacy', *Business Ethics Quarterly,* Vol.7(2), pp.31-44.

Dunfee, T W (1996), *Ethical challenges of managing across cultures*, Invited plenary paper presented at the Ninth Annual European Business Ethics Networks Conference, Seeheim, Germany.

Dunfee, T W (1991), 'Business Ethics and extant social contracts', *Business Ethics Quarterly,* Vol.1(1), pp.23-51.

Dunfee, T W and T Donaldson (1995), 'Contractarian business ethics: Current status and next steps', *Business Ethics Quarterly,* Vol.5(2), pp.173-186.

Dunleavy, P and B O'Leary (1987), *Theories of the state: The Politics of Liberal Democracy*, Macmillan Education.

Dunn, J (1984), *Locke*, Oxford University Press.

Edey, H C (1984), 'Company Accounting in the Nineteenth and Twentieth Centuries', in Lee, T A & R H Parker, (1984) (eds.) *The Evolution of Corporate Financial Reporting'*, pp.222-230, Garland Publishing Inc. New York & London.

Elkington, J (1999), *Cannibals with Forks: The Triple Bottom Line of 21ˢᵗ Century Business*, Capstone, Oxford.

Elkington, J and S Fennell (2000), 'Partners for sustainability', in Bendell, J (ed.) *Terms for Endearment: Business, NGOs and Sustainable Development,* Greenleaf, Sheffield.

Enderle, G (1996), 'A Comparison of Business Ethics in North America and Continental Europe', *Business Ethics: A European Review,* Vol.5, No.1, pp.33-46.

Enderle, G (1995), *What is international? A topology of international spheres and its relevance for business ethics*, Paper presented at annual meeting of the Association of Business and Society, Vienna, Austria.

Enteman, W F (2001), 'Contextualising Business Ethics', *Business and Society Review*, Vol.106, No.2, pp.143-160.

Epstein, E M (2002), 'Religion and Business – The Critial Role of Religious Traditions in Management Education', *Journal of Business Ethics'*, Vol.38, pp.91-96.

Epstein, E M (1989), 'Business Ethics, Corporate Good Citizenship and the Corporate Social Policy Process: A View from the United States', *Journal of Business Ethics,* August.

Epstein, E M (1977), 'The Social Role of Business Enterprise in Britain: An American perspective; Part II, *Journal of Management Studies,* Vol.14, No.3, pp.281-316.

Epstein, E M (1976), 'The Social Role of Business Enterprise in Britain: An American perspective; Part I, *Journal of Management Studies,* Vol.13, No.3, pp.213-33.

Escobar, L (1975), 'Should there be an International regulatory Agency for MNCs?' in Gunnemann, J P (ed) (1975), The Nation-State and Transnational Corporations in Conflict with special reference to Latin America, Praeger Publishers, New York.

Etzioni, A (1988), *The Moral Dimension: Toward a new economics,* The Free Press, New York.

Evan, W M and R E Freeman (1993), 'A stakeholder theory of the modern corporation: Kantain capitalism', in Hoffman W M and R E Frederick (eds.), *Business Ethics: Readings and Cases in Corporate Morality,* 3rd edition, McGraw-Hill, New York.

Evan, W M and R E Freeman (1988), 'A stakeholder theory of the modern corporation: Kantain capitalism', in Beauchamp, T L and N E Bowie (eds.), *Ethical theory and business,* (3rd edition), Prentice Hall, Englewood Cliffs, NJ.

Evans, P and T Wurster (2000), *Blown to Bits,* Tree Press, New York.

Fisher, C and A Lovell (2003), *Business Ethics and Values*, FT Prentice Hall.

Flew, A (1961), *Hume's Philosophy of Belief,* Routledge & Kegan Paul.

Fogarty, M (1975), 'Company Responsibility and Participation: A New Agenda', *PEP Broadsheet*, Vol.41, No.554, P.E.P. London.

Frank, R and P Cook (1995), *The Winner-Take-All Society: How More and More Americans Compete for Ever Fewer and Bigger Prizes, Encouraging Economic Waste, Income, Inequality, and an Impoverished Cultural Life*, Free Press, New York.

Franklin Research and Development Corporation, (1992), *Human Rights: Investing for a Better World*, Boston, MA.

Franklin, B (1996/1785), Autobiography, *The Works of Benjamin Franklin, 1731-5*, Putnams, New York.

Freeman, R E (1984), *Strategic management: A stakeholder approach*, Pitman, Boston, MA.

Friedman, M (1970), 'The social responsibility of Business is to increase its profits', *New York Times Magazine*, 13 September, Vol.33, pp.122–126

Friedman, M and R Friedman (1980), *Free to Choose: A Personal Statement*, Secker and Warburg, London.

Friedman, M and R Friedman (1962), *Capitalism and Freedom*, Chicago University Press, Chicago.

Galbraith, J K (1958), *The Affluent Society*, Hamish Hamilton, London.

Gautschi, F H and T M Jones (1987), 'Illegal Corporate Behaviour and Corporate Board Structure', Research in *Corporate Social Performance and Policy: Empirical Studies of Business Ethics and Values*, Vol.9.

Gilpin, R (2002), 'A Realist Perspective on International Governance', in (eds.) Held, D and A Mcgrew, *Governing Globalization: Power, Authority and Global Governance*, Polity.

Glover, J (2001), *Humanity: A moral history of the twentieth century*, Pimlico.

Gonella, C, A Pilling and S Zadek (1998), *Making Values Count*, (research report 57 from the Association of Chartered Certified Accountants; London, Certified Accountants Educational Trust).

Goodpaster, K (1983), 'The Concept of Corporate Responsibility', *Journal of Business Ethics*, February.

Goodpaster, K E (2002), Foreword, in (eds.) Cortright, S A and M J Naughton (2002), *Rethinking the Purpose of Business*, p.ix-xii, University of Notre Dame, Indiana.

Goodpaster, K E (2000), 'The Caux Round table Principles: Corporate Moral Reflection in a Global Business Environment', in (ed.) Williams, O F, *Global Codes of Conduct: An Idea Whose Time Has Come*, Notre Dame, Ind, University of Notre Dame Press, pp.183-195.

Goodwin, B (1987), *Using Political Ideas*, 2nd edition, John Wiley & Sons Limited.

Gottlieb, A (2001), *The Dream of Reason: A History of Philosophy from the Greeks to the Renaissance,* Penguin Books.

Goyder, G (1961), *The Responsible Company,* Oxford University Press.

Goyder, G (1951), *The Future of Private Enterprise*, Oxford University Press.

Gray, J (1989), *Liberalisms: Essays in Political Philosophy*, Routledge, London.

Gray, R H (1992), 'Accounting and environmentalism: an exploration of the challenge of gently accounting for accountability, transparency and sustainability', *Accounting, Organizations and Society,* Vol.17, No.5, pp.399-426.

Green, M (2002), *But don't all religions lead to God?: navigating the multi-faith maze*, Inter-Varsity Press.

Green, R M (1997), 'Guiding principles of Jewish business ethics, *Business Ethics Quarterly,* Vol.7(2), pp.21-30.

Greenspan, A (1998), 'Is There a New Economy?', *California Management Review,* Vol.41, No.1, pp.74-85.

Gunnemann, J P (ed) (1975), *The Nation-State and Transnational Corporations in Conflict with special reference to Latin America*, Praeger Publishers, New York.

Habermas, J (1993), *Justification and Application; Remarks of Discourse Ethics,* translated by C Cronin, MIT Press, Cambridge, MA.

Handy, C (1996), *The Empty Raincoat: making sense of the future,* Hutchinson, London.

Harvey, B (ed.) (1994), *Business Ethics: A European Approach*, Prentice Hall.

Hayek, F A von (1976), *Individualism and Economic Order*, Routledge & Kegan Paul, London.

Hayek, F A von (1973), *Law, Legislation and Liberty: A new statement of the liberal principles of justice and political economy*, Routledge and Kegan Paul, London.

Hayek, F A von (1960), *The Constitution of Liberty,* University of Chicago Press, Chicago.

Hayek, F A von (1944), *The Road to Serfdom,* Routledge, London.

Heidegger, M (1959), *An Introduction to Metaphysics*, translated by R Manheim, Yale University Press.

Heidegger, M (translation and introduction by D F Krell) (1978), *Basic writings from 'Being and time' (1927 to 'The task of thinking, 1964),* Routledge and Kegan Paul, London.

Held, D (2002), 'Cosmopolitanism: Ideas, Realities and Deficits', in (eds.) Held, D and A Mcgrew, *Governing Globalization: Power, Authority and Global Governance*, Polity.

Held, D (1987), *Models of Democracy,* Polity Press, Cambridge.

Higgs, D (2003), *Review of the Role and Effectiveness of Non-Executive Directors*, Department of Trade and Industry, London.

Himmelfarb, G (1974), *On Liberty and Liberalism: The case of John Stuart Mill,* Knopf.

Hirsch, F (1977), *Social Limits to Growth*, Routledge & Kegan Paul, London.

Hirshman, A O (1996), 'Rival Interpretations of Market society: Civilizing, Destructive or Feeble?' in (ed.) Castro, B (1996) *Business & Society: A Reader in the History, Sociology and Ethics of Business*, Oxford University Press, New York.

Hobbes, T (1998) 'Leviathan or the Matter, Form and Power of a Commonwealth Ecclesiastical and Civil', in (ed.) L P Pojman, 'Classics of Philosophy', pp.491-528, Oxford University Press, New York.

Hobbes, T (1968), *Leviathan,* Penguin, Harmondsworth.

Hoffman, W M (1988), *Business Ethics in the United States: Its Past Decade and its Future,* Bentley College, Mass.

Hoffman, W M and J M Moore (1984), *Business Ethics: Readings and Cases in Corporate Morality,* McGraw-Hill.

Hofstede, G (1980), *Cultural Consequences,* Sage, Beverly Hills, CA.

Holland, L and J Gibbon (2001), 'Processes in social and ethical accountability: External reporting mechanisms', in J Andriof and M McIntosh (eds.) (2001), *Perspectives on Corporate Citizenship,* Greenleaf Publishing Limited.

Hughes, H S (1979), *Consciousness & Society: The reorientation of European Social Thought 1890-1930,* The Harvester Press.

Hull, G and L Peikoff (eds.) (1999), *The Ayn Rand Reader,* Penguin, New York.

Humble, J (1976), 'Social Responsibility: The Heart of Business', *Unilever Topics,* No.4, Nov/Dec, 1a-2a,

Husserl, E (1965), *Phenomenology and the Crisis of Philosophy,* (translated by Q Lauer), Harper & Rowe, New York.

Husserl, E (1931), *Ideas: A general introduction to Pure Phenomenology,* (translated by W R Boyce-Gibson), George Allen & Unwin Ltd, London.

Hutchinson, T W (1981), *The Politics and Philosophy of Economics: Marxians, Keynesians and Austrians,* Basil Blackwell, Oxford.

Hutton, W (2002), *The World We're In,* Brown, Little.

Ivens, M (ed) (1970), *Industry and Values: The Objectives and Responsibilities of Business,* Harrop, London.

Jacks, L P (1924), 'The Challenge of Life', Hibbert Lectures, Hodder and Staughton, London.

Jeremy, D J (1990), *Capitalists and Christians: Business Leaders and the Churches in Britain, 1900-1960*, OUP, Oxford.

Jones, D J (1977), *A Bibliography of Business Ethics, 1971-1975*, University of Virginia Press.

Jones, T (1995), 'Instrumental stakeholder theory: Synthesis of ethics and economics, *Academy of Management Review,* Vol.20(2), pp.404-437.

Joseph, K (1976), *Stranded on the Middle Ground*, Centre for Policy Studies; London.

Kell, G (2004), *Gearing Up: From Corporate Governance to Good Governance and Scalable Solutions*, Foreword, AccountAbility.

Kelly, K (1998), *New Rules for the New Economy,* Penguin Books, New York.

Kempner, T, K MacMillan and K Hawkins (1974), *Business and Society: Tradition and Change*, Allen Lane, London.

Keniston, K (1986), 'The Alienating Consequences of Capitalist Technology', in (eds.) Edwards, R C, M Reich and T E Weisskopf (1986), *The Capitalist System,* pp.269-273, Prentice-Hall, Englewood Cliffs, N.J.

Klein, S (1985), 'Two views of Business Ethics: A popular philosophical approach and a value-based interdisciplinary one', *Journal of Business Ethics*, Kluckhorn, C (1955), 'Ethical relativity: Sic et non', *Journal of Philosophy*, Vol.52, pp.663-677.

Kolk, A and R V Tulder (2002), 'Child Labor and Multinational Conduct; A Comparison of International Business and Stakeholder Codes', *Journal of Business Ethics*, Vol.36, pp.291-301.

Kolk, A, R V Tulder and C Welters (1999), 'International Codes of Conduct and Corporate Social Responsibility: Can Transnational Corporations Regulate Themselves?', *Transnational Corporations*, Vol.8(1), pp.143-180.

Kristol, I (1973), 'Capitalism, Socialism and Nihilism', *The Public Interest,* Spring, p.13.

La Croix, W (1976), *Principles for Ethics in Business*, University Press of America.

Ladd, J (1970), 'Morality and the Ideal of Rationality in Formal Organizations', *Monist*, Vol.54, No.4.

Lee, T A (1984), 'Company Financial Statements: An Essay in Business History 1830-1950', in Lee, T A and R H Parker (1984) (eds.) *The Evolution of Corporate Financial Reporting*, pp.15-29, Garland Publishing Inc. New York & London.

Lee, T A and R H Parker (1984), *The Evolution of Corporate Financial Reporting*, Garland Publishing Inc. New York and London.

Lessnoff, M (1986), *Social Contract*, Macmillan.

Levine, A (1987), *Economics and Jewish Law*, Ktav & Yeshiva University Press, New York.

Levitt, T (1956), 'The Lonely Crowd and the Economic Man', *Quarterly Journal of Economics*, February, p.109.

Liedtka, J (2002), 'Ethics and the New Economy', *Business sand Society Review*, Vol.107, No.1, pp.1-19.

Lindblom, C E (1977), *Politics and Markets: The World's Political-Economic Systems*, Basic Books Inc.

Ling, T (1968), 'A History of Religion East and West', Macmillan.

Litvin, D (2003), *Empires of Profit: Commerce, Conquest and Corporate Responsibility*, TEXERE LLC, New York.

Locke, J (1952), *The Second Treatise of Government*, The Library of Liberal Arts.

Lodge, G C (1982), 'The Connections between Ethics and Ideology', *Journal of Business Ethics*, May.

Lovell, A (2002), 'Moral Agency as Victim of the Vulnerability of Autonomy', *Business Ethics: A European Review*, Vol.11, No.1, pp.62-76.

Luthans, F, R M Hodgetts and K R Thompson (1987), *Social Issues in Business: Strategic and Public Policy Perspectives*, Macmillan Publishing Company, New York.

McDonald, G and A Nijhof (1999), 'Beyond codes of ethics: an integrated framework for stimulating morally responsible behaviour in organisations', *Leadership & Organisation Development Journal,* Vol.20(3), pp.133-146.

McGrew, A (2002), 'Liberal Internationalism: Between realism and Cosmopolitanism', in (eds.) D Held and A Mcgrew, *Governing Globalization: Power, Authority and Global Governance,* Polity.

McHugh, F P (1988), *Keyguide to Information Sources in Business Ethics,* Nichols Publishing.

McIntosh, M, R Thomas, D Leipziger and G Coleman (2003), *Living Corporate Citizenship: Strategic routes to socially responsible business,* FT Prentice Hall.

MacIntyre, A (1981), *After Virtue, A Study in Moral Theory,* Duckworth, London.

MacIntyre, A (1977), *Why are the problems of Business Ethics Insoluble?,* Bentley College, Mass.

MacIntyre, A (ed.) (1972), *Hegel: A Collection of Critical Essays,* University of Notre Dame Press.

MacIntyre, A (1967), *A Short History of Ethics: A History of Moral Philosophy from the Homeric Age to the Twentieth Century,* Routledge, London.

McLellan, D (1973), *Karl Marx: His Life and Thought,* Harper & Row.

McMylor, P (1994), *Alistair MacIntyre: Critic of Modernity,* Routledge, London.

Mahoney, J (1990), *Teaching Business Ethics in the UK, Europe and the USA: A Comparative Study,* The Athlone Press.

Maignan, I (2001), 'Consumers perceptions of corporate social responsibilities: a cross-cultural comparison', *Journal of Business Ethics,* Vol.30(1/1), pp.57-72.

Maignan, I and O C Ferrell (2000), 'Measuring corporate citizenship in two countries: the case of the United states and France', *Journal of Business Ethics,* Vol.23, pp.283-97.

Maignan, I and O C Ferrell (2001), 'Antecedents and benefits of corporate citizenship: an investigation of French businesses', *Journal of Business Research*, Vol.51, pp.37-51.

Maignan, I, O C Ferrell and G T M Hult (1999), 'Corporate Citizenship: cultural antecedents and business benefits', *Journal of the Academy of Marketing Science*, Vol.27/4, pp.455-69.

Mannheim, K (1936), *Ideology and Utopia*, translated by L Wirth and E Shils, Harcourt, Brace & World, New York.

Marinetto, M (1999), 'The Historical Development of Business Philanthropy: Social Responsibility in the New Corporate Economy', *Business History*, Vol.41, No.4, pp.1-20.

Marshall, G (1982), *In search of the spirit of capitalism: An essay on Max Weber's Protestant ethic thesis*, Gregg Revivals, Hutchinson & Co.

Mates, B (1983), *The Philosophy of Leibnitz: Metaphysics and Language*, Oxford University Press.

Matthews, J B, K E Goodpaster and L N Nash (1991), 'Environmental Pressures: The Pollution Problem', in (2nd edition), *Policies and Persons: A Casebook in Business Ethics*, pp.414-433, McGraw-Hill.

Matthews, J B, K E Goodpaster and L N Nash (1985), *Policies and Persons: A Casebook in Business Ethics*, 2nd edition, pp.414-433, McGraw-Hill Inc.

Meadows, D H, D L Meadows, J Randers and W W Behrens (1974), *The Limits to Growth*, Pan, London.

Mescon, T S and G S Vozikis (1984), 'Hooker Chemical and the Love Canal', in (eds.) W M Hoffman and J M Moore (1984), *Business Ethics: Readings and Cases in Corporate Morality*, 2nd. Edition, pp.592-597, McGraw-Hill Publishing Company.

Messner, J (1952), *Social Ethics*, translated from the German by J J Doherty, B Herder, St. Louis.

Miceli, M P and J P Near (1992), *Blowing the Whistle: The Organizational & Legal Implications for Companies and Employees*, Lexington Books.

Micklethwait, J and A Wooldridge (2003), *The Company: A Short History of a Revolutionary Idea*, Weidenfeld & Nicolson, London.

Mill, J S (1998), *On Liberty and other Essays*, (ed.) J Gray, Oxford University Press, Oxford.

Mill, J S (1971), *Utilitarianism*, (reprint of 1861 edition), Penguin, Harmondsworth.

Mill, J S (1970/1848), *Principles of Political Economy*, Book IV, Chapter VI, Penguin, Harmondsworth.

Mitchell, N J (1989), *The Generous Corporation: A Political Analysis of Corporate Power*, Yale University Press, New Haven CT.

Mitchell, R K, B R Agle and D J Wood (1997), 'Toward a theory of stakeholder identification and salience: Defining the principle of who and what really counts', *Academy of Management Review*, Vol.22(4), pp.853-886.

Monks, R A G (2003), 'Equity Culture at Risk: The Threat to Anglo-American Prosperity', *Corporate Governance: An International Review*, Vol.11, No.3, July, pp.164-170.

Nash, L and S McLennan (2001), *Church on Sunday, Work on Monday*, Jossey-Bass, San Frncisco.

Nelson, B N (1949), *The Idea of Usury, from Tribal Brotherhood to Universal Otherhood*, Princeton University Press, Princeton.

Newberry, W E and T N Gladwin (2002), 'Shell and Nigerian Oil', in Donaldson, T, P H Werhane and M Cording (eds.) *Ethical Issues in Business: A Philosophical Approach*, pp.522-540, Prentice Hall, N.J.

Niebuhr, R (1932), *Moral Man and Immoral Society*, C Scribner, New York.

Nietzsche, F (1973), *Beyond Good and Evil*, (trans. R J Hollingdale), Penguin Classics.

Nisbet, R A (1953), *The Quest for Community*, Oxford University Press, Oxford.

Noonan, J T Jr. (1957), *The scholastic analysis of Usury*, Harvard University Press, Cambridge.

Nozick, R (1974), *Anarchy, State and Utopia*, Basic Books, New York.

O'Sullivan, M A (2001), *Contests for Corporate Control: Corporate governance and economic performance in the United States and Germany*, Oxford University Press, Oxford.

Oakeshott, M (1983), *On History and Other Essays*, Barnes & Noble Books, New Jersey.

Oakeshott, M (1975), *On Human Conduct*, Clarendon Press, Oxford.

Oakeshott, M (1962), *Rationalism in Politics*, Methuen, London.

Oestreich, J E (2002), 'What can businesses do to appease anti-globalization protestors?', *Business and Society Review*, Vol.107, No.2, pp.207-220.

Orwig, S F (2002), 'Business Ethics and the Protestant Spirit: How Norman Vincent Peale Shaped the Religious Values of American Business Leaders', *Journal of Business Ethics*, Vol.38, pp.81-89.

Owen, D (1995), *Nietzsche, Politics & Modernity*, Sage Publications.

Pateman, C (1985), *The Problem of Political Obligation: A Critique of Liberal Theory*, John Wiley & Sons.

Pearce, D (1999), *Economics and Environment: Essays on Ecological Economics and Sustainable Development*, Edward Elgar, Cheltenham.

Perri 6, 'Global Digital Communications and the Prospects for Transnational Regulation', in (eds.), Held, D and A McGrew, 2002, Governing Globalization, Polity.

Peters, R (1956), *Hobbes*, Penguin.

Phelps, E S (ed) (1975), *Altruism, Morality and Economic Theory*, Sage Foundation, New York.

Pilger, J (2003), 'What good friends left behind', *The Guardian Weekend Magazine*, 20 September, pp.43-49.

Pilger, J (2001), 'Spoils of a massacre', *Guardian Weekend*, 14 July, pp.18-29.

Plant, R (1992), *Enterprise in its place: the moral limits of markets*, in Heelas P and P Morris (eds.) *The Values of the Enterprise Culture: The Moral Debate,* pp.85-99, Routledge.

Plato (1935), *The Republic*, Dent.

Pojman, L P (1998), *Classics of Philosophy*, Oxford University Press, Oxford.

Poole, R (1991), *Morality and Modernity*, Routledge, London.

Porter, M E and M R Kramer (2002), 'The Competitive Advantage of Corporate Philanthropy', *Harvard Business Review*, pp.56-68, December.

Powers, C W (1975), 'Interdependence and Corporate Decision-Making: Three Kinds of Interdependence and the Space for Ethical Choice', in Gunnemann, J P (ed.), (1975), *The Nation-State and Transnational Corporations in Conflict with special reference to Latin America*, Praeger Publishers, New York.

Prakash, A (2000), 'Responsible Care: An Assessment', *Business and Society*, Vol.39(2), pp.183-209.

Rand, A (2001), (website) http://www.geocities.com/AthensAegean/1311/rand.html

Rand, A (1999), *The Ayn Rand Reader*, (ed.) Hull, G and L Peikoff, Plume Books, Harmondsworth.

Rae, J (1895), *Life of Adam Smith,* Letter 150.

Raphael, D D and A L Macfie (1976), *Adam Smith: The Theory of Moral Sentiments*, Oxford University Press, London.

Rawls, J (1999), *A Theory of Justice*, Revised edition, Oxford University Press.

Rawls, J (1971), *A Theory of Justice*, Oxford University Press.

Reich, R (1998), 'The New meaning of Corporate Social Responsbility', *California Management Review*, Vol.40, No.2, pp.8-17.

Reich, R B (1996), *Pink Slips, Profits and Paychecks: Corporate Citizenship in an era of smaller government*, address at George Washington University School of Business and Public Management, 6 February.

Robertson, J (1974), *Profit or People: The New Social Role of Money*, Calder Boyars, London.

Rodgers, D T (1974), *The Work Ethic in Industrial America*, The University of Chicago Press and London, Chicago.

Roe, M (1994), *Strong Managers, Weak Owners: The Political Roots of American Corporate Finance*, Princeton, N.J.

Rose, H and S Rose (eds.) (2000), *Alas, Poor Darwin: Arguments against evolutionary psychology*, Jonathon Cape, London.

Rose, C and C Mejer (2003), 'The Danish Corporate Governance System: from stakeholder orientation towards shareholder value', *Corporate Governance,* Vol.11, No.4, pp.335-344.

Rosenau, J N (2002), 'Governance in a New Global Order', in (eds.) Held, D and A Mcgrew, *Governing Globalization: Power, Authority and Global Governance*, Polity.

Ross, W D (1930), *The Right and the Good*, Clarendon Press, Oxford.

Rousseau, J-J (1913), *The Social Contract*, J M Dent & Sons Ltd, London.

Ruff, L E (1985), 'The Economic Common Sense of Pollution' in (eds.) Hoffman, W M and J M Moore (1984), *Business Ethics: Readings and Cases in Corporate Morality*, 2nd. Edition, pp.487-493, McGraw-Hill Publishing Company.

Russell, B (1900), *A Critical Exposition of the Philosophy of Leibnitz*, George Aleen & Unwin.

Sarason, S B (1986), 'And what is the public interest?', *American Psychologist,* August.

Satchell, M J (1994), *Deadly trade in toxics, US News & World Report*, 7 March, pp.64, 66, 68.

Sawyer, G C (1979), *Business and society: Managing Corporate Social Impact*, Houghton Mifflin Company, Boston.

Schlesinger (n.d.), 'Epilogue: The One Against the Many', in Schlesinger and White, *Paths of American Thought*.

Schnall, D J (1993), 'Exploratory notes on employee productivity and accountability in classic Jewish sources', *Journal of Business Ethics*, Vol.12, pp.485-491.

Schumpeter, J A (1976), *Capitalism. Socialism and Democracy*, 5th edition, George Allen & Unwin.

Seedhouse, D (1988), *Ethics: The Heart of Health Care,* John Wiley & Sons, New York.

Sell, S K (2002), 'Intellectual Property Rights', in (eds.) Held, D and A Mcgrew, *Governing Globalization: Power, Authority and Global Governance*, Polity.

Sen, A (1999), *Development as Freedom,* Alfred A Knopf, New York.

Sen, A (1985), 'The Standard of Living; Lecture I, Concepts and Critiques', in Sen, A (ed), *The Standard of Living*, Cambridge University Press.

Sennett, R (1998), *The Corrosion of Character: The Personal Consequences of Work in the New Capitalism*, W W Norton, New York.

Shapiro, C and H Varian (1999), *Information Rules,* Harvard Business School, Boston.

Shaw, W H and V Barry (1998), *Moral issues in Business*, 7th edition, Wadsworth Publishing Company, Belmont, Calif.

Shenfield, B (1971), *Company Boards; Their Responsibilities to Shareholders, Employees and the Community,* Allen & Unwin, London.

Silverman, H J (ed.) (1988), 'Philosophy and Non-Philosopgy since Merleau-Ponty', Routledge.

Silverman, H J, A Mickunas, T Kisiel and A Lingis (1988), *The Horizons of Continental Philosophy*, Kluwer Academic Publishers, Dordrecht.

Singer, P (1983), *Hegel*, Oxford University Press, Oxford.

Singer, P (1980), *Marx,* Oxford University Press, Oxford.

Singh, K (1992), *Sikhism For Modern Man*, Guru Nanak Dev University.

Skorecki, A and S Targett (2001), 'Ethical index bars top UK groups, *Financial Times*, 11 July.

Slapper, G and S Tombs (1999), *Corporate Crime*, Longman.

Smith, A (1759/1976), *The Theory of Moral Sentiments, (*eds) Raphael, D D and A L Macfie, Clarendon Press, Oxford.

Smith, A (1766/1976), *An Inquiry into the Nature and Causes of the Wealth of Nations*, with an introduction by A Skinner, Penguin Books.

Solomon, R C (1992), *Ethics and Excellence: Cooperation and Integrity in Business*, Oxford University Press, New York.

Soros, G (2000), *Open Society: Reforming Global Capitalism*, Brown, Little.

Spaemann R (1989), *Basic Moral Concepts*, (translated by T J Armstrong), Routledge.

Spencer, H (1892), *The Principles of Ethics*, Vols I, II and III, D Appleton and Company, New York.

Spencer, H (1862), *First Principles*, Williams and Norgate, London.

Spencer, H (1857), 'Progress: its law and cause', *The Leader*, 20 March, Reprinted in Spencer (1892, Vol. I, pp.1-59).

SSRC (Social Science Research Council) (1976), *The Social Responsibilities of Business*, A Report to the Social Science Research Council by an SSRC Advisory Panel, London:

Steiner, G A (1975), *Business and Society*, 2nd edition, Random House.

Steiner, G A and J F Steiner (1977), *Issues in Business and Society*, 2nd edition, Random House.

Stewart, T (1998), 'Knowledge, the Appreciating Commodity', *Fortune*, Vol.138, No.7, pp.199-200.

Stiglitz, J (2003), *The Roaring Nineties: Seeds of destruction*, Allen Lane.

Stiglitz, J (2002), *Globalization and its discontents*, Penguin.

Stiglitz, J E (2000), 'Failure of the Fund', *Harvard International Review*, Summer, pp.14-26.

SustainAbility (2004), *Gearing Up: From corporate responsibility to good governance and scalable solutions*, UN Global Compact, New York.

Tamari, M (1987), *With All Your Possessions: Jewish Ethics & Economic Life*, The Free Press, New York.

Tawney, R H (1966), *Religion and the Rise of Capitalism*, Penguin, Harmondsworth.

Thomson, J W (2002), 'The Future of Globalisation', *Business and Society*, Vol.107, No.4, pp.423-431.

Thurrow, L (1982), *The Zero-Sum Society*, Penguin, New York.

Titmuss, R (1970), *The Gift Relationship: From Human Blood to Social Policy*, Allen & Unwin, London.

Tocqueville, A (1946), *Democracy in America,* (trans. H Reeve), Oxford University Press.

Tucker, R (ed.) (1978), *The Marx-Engels Reader,* Norton.

Turner, C H and A Trompenaars (1993), *The seven deadly cultures of capitalism*, Doubleday, New York.

Turner, J (1985), *Herbert Spencer: A renewed Appreciation*, Sage Publications, Beverly Hills, CA.

Van Luijk, H J L (1990), 'Recent Developments in Business Ethics', *Journal of Business Ethics*, Vol.9, pp.537-544.

Vickers, L (2002), *Freedom of Speech and Employment*, Oxford Monographs on Labour Law, Oxford University Press.

Viereck, P (1953), *Shame and Glory of the Intellectuals*, Beacon, Boston.

Vogel, D (1998), 'Is US business obsessed with ethics?', *Across the Board*, November-December, pp.31-33.

Vogel, D (1992), 'The globalization of business ethics: why America remains different', *California Management Review*, Vol.35, No.1, pp.30-49.

Waddell, S (2000), 'New institutions for the practice of corporate citizenship: historical, intersectoral, and developmental perspectives', *Business and Society Review*, Vol.105, No.1, pp.107-126.

Waddock, S (2001), 'Integrity and mindfulness: foundations of corporate citizenship', in Andriof J and M McIntosh (eds.) (2001), *Perspectives on Corporate Citizenship*, Greenleaf Publishing Limited.

Walzer, M (1983), *Spheres of Justice,* Martin Robertson, Oxford.

Weber, M (1985), *The Protestant Work Ethic and the Rise of Capitalism*, trans. Talcott Parsons, Allen and Unwin, London.

Weber, M (1968), *Economy and Society*, Bedminster Press, New York.

Weick, K E (1995), *Sensemaking in Organisations*, Sage Publications.

Weiss, J W (1998), *Business Ethics: A Stakeholder and Issues Management Approach*, 2nd. Edition, The Dryden Press.

Werhane, P H (2002), 'Business Ethics and the Origins of Contemporary Capitalism: Economics and Ethics in the work of Adam Smith and Herbert Spencer', in (ed.) Frederick, R.E. *A Companion to Business Ethics*, Blackwell Publishing.

Whyte, W H Jr. (1956), *The Organizational Man*, Simon and Schuster, New York.

Williams, B (1985), 'The Standard of Living: Interests and Capabilities', in Sen, A. (ed) *The Standard of Living*, Cambridge University Press.

Williams, G L (1976), *John Stuart Mill on Politics and Society*, Fontana.

Windsor, D (2001), 'Corporate Citizenship, Evolution and interpretation', in Andriof. J and M McIntosh (eds.) (2001), *Perspectives on Corporate Citizenship*, pp.39-52, Greenleaf Publishing Limited.

Wolf, M (2000), 'Sleepwalking with the Enemy: Corporate Social Responsibility Distorts the Market by Deflecting Business from its Primary Role of Profit Generation', *Financial Times*, 16 May, p.21.

Wood, D J and J M Logsdon (2001), 'Theorising Business Citizenship', in (eds.) Andriof. J and M McIntosh, M (eds.) (2001), *Perspectives on Corporate Citizenship*, pp.83-103, Greenleaf Publishing Limited.

Woods, N (2002), 'Global Governance and the Role of Institutions', in (eds.) Held, D and A Mcgrew, *Governing Globalization: Power, Authority and Global Governance*, Polity.

Zadek, S (2001a), 'Partnership, alchemy: engagement, innovation and governance', in (eds.) Andriof. J and M McIntosh (eds.), *Perspectives on Corporate Citizenship*, pp.200-214, Greenleaf Publishing Limited.

Zadek, S (2001b), *The Civil Corporation: the new economy of corporate citizenship*, Earthscan Publications, London.

Zadek, S, P Pruzan and R Evans (1997), *Building Corporate Accountability*, Earthscan Publications Ltd, London.